Mediterranean Diet: The Essential Beginners Guide To Quick Weight Loss And Healthy Living
Plus Over 100 Delicious Quick and Easy Recipes + 7 Day Meal Plan

Alberto Benetti

© **Copyright 2016 Alberto Benetti All rights reserved.**

This document is geared towards providing exact and reliable information in regards to the topic and issue covered. The publication is sold with the idea that the publisher is not required to render accounting, officially permitted, or otherwise, qualified services. If advice is necessary, legal or professional, a practiced individual in the profession should be ordered.

- From a Declaration of Principles which was accepted and approved equally by a Committee of the American Bar Association and a Committee of Publishers and Associations.

In no way is it legal to reproduce, duplicate, or transmit any part of this document in either electronic means or in printed format. Recording of this publication is strictly prohibited and any storage of this document is not allowed unless with written permission from the publisher. All rights reserved.

The information provided herein is stated to be truthful and consistent, in that any liability, in terms of inattention or otherwise, by any usage or abuse of any policies, processes, or directions contained within is the solitary and utter responsibility of the recipient reader. Under no circumstances will any legal responsibility or blame be held against the publisher for any reparation, damages, or monetary loss due to the information herein, either directly or indirectly.

Respective authors own all copyrights not held by the publisher. The information herein is offered for informational purposes solely, and is universal as so. The presentation of the information is without contract or any type of guarantee assurance.

The trademarks that are used are without any consent, and the publication of the trademark is without permission or backing by the trademark owner. All trademarks and brands within this book are for clarifying purposes only and are the owned by the owners themselves, not affiliated with this document.

The material on this book is for informational purposes only. As each individual situation is unique, you should use proper discretion, in consultation with a health care practitioner, before undertaking the protocols, diet, exercises, techniques, training methods, or otherwise described herein. The author and publisher expressly disclaim responsibility for any adverse effects that may result from the use or application of the information contained herein.

Table of contents

Introduction	8
Chapter 1: How Your Diet and Lifestyle are Slowly Killing You	9
Chapter 2: The Mediterranean Diet Revealed	14
Chapter 3: Unlock the Mediterranean Lifestyle	18
Chapter 4: Is the Mediterranean Diet Right for Me?	28
Chapter 5: The Mediterranean Diet Essentials	36
Chapter 6: Putting the Mediterranean Diet to Use In Your Daily Life	44
Chapter 7: Going Out to Eat on the Mediterranean Diet	48
Chapter 8: Making the Choice to Follow the Mediterranean Diet	50
102 Delicious Mediterranean Recipes	53
Breakfast	53
Egg Omelet from the Oven	53
Spinach Frittata	54
Blueberry Quinoa	55
Peanut Butter Banana Yogurt Bowl	56
Egg Muffins with Vegetables and Parmesan Cheese	57
Couscous with Apricots and Pistachios	58
Baked Eggs from Tuscany	59
Breakfast Vegetarian Sandwich	60
Sandwiches	61
Panera Mediterranean Veggie Sandwich	61
Grilled Veggie Sandwich	62
Sandwich Loaded with Green Veggies	63
Mediterranean Picnic Sandwich	64
Classic Pita Sandwich	65
Grilled Turkey Sandwich	66
Tuna Sandwich with Hummus	67
Chicken Sandwich	68

Super Simple Tuna Sandwich	69
Avocado Tuna Sandwich	70
Tuna Sandwich with Walnuts	71
Quick Chicken Pita Sandwich	72
Chicken Sandwich with Goat Cheese	73
Chicken Pita Sandwich	74
Chicken	75
Stuffed Chicken	75
Chicken Breasts with Mozzarella	76
Simple Oven Chicken	77
Grilled Chicken Breasts	78
Greek Lemon Chicken	79
Chicken Tomato Soup	80
Chicken with Polenta	81
Quick Chicken with Vegetables	82
Chicken from a Skillet	83
Garlic Lemon Herb Chicken	84
Chicken with Basil Risotto	85
Roasted Chicken, Potatoes and Peppers	86
Creamy Risotto with Chicken	87
Chicken with Couscous	89
Quinoa Chicken with Feta Cheese	90
Simple Chicken from the Oven	91
Baked Chicken with Potatoes	92
Chicken with Orzo Pasta	93
Lemon Grilled Chicken	94
Casseroles	95
Chicken Casserole with Mushrooms	95
Vegetarian Zucchini Casserole	96
Rigatoni and Cheese Casserole	97
Egg Casserole with Artichokes	98

Glazed Chicken Casserole	99
Kale Quinoa Casserole	100
Rice and Bean Casserole	101
Fish	102
Lemon Orzo Shrimp	102
Microwave Fish with Green Beans	103
Roasted Salmon with Rice	104
Quick and Easy Baked Fish	105
Baked Tilapia with Feta Cheese	106
Swordfish with Tomatoes	107
Fish Stew with Prawns	108
Salmon with Vegetable Quinoa	109
Baked Halibut with Artichokes	110
Tilapia with Vegetables	111
Pappardelle with Red Mullet	112
Sardine Escabeche	113
Halibut Fillets with Fennel	114
Simple Mediterranean Cod	115
Simple Mediterranean Salmon	116
Baked Salmon in Tin Foil	117
Oven Baked Trout	118
Oven Baked Halibut	119
Oven Baked Branzino	120
Trout with Olives and Fennel	121
Pasta	122
Pasta with Artichokes, Olives, and Tomatoes	122
Pasta Salad with Feta and Parmesan	123
Pasta with Zucchini	124
Pasta with Eggplant and Pine Kernels	125
Spaghetti with Chorizo	126
Chicken with Penne Pasta	127

Greek Vegetarian Pasta	128
Baked Pasta with Shrimp	129
Oven Baked Pasta	130
Side Dishes	131
Baked Risotto with Chorizo Sausage	131
Vegetarian Mushroom Risotto	132
Vegetable Chili	133
Eggplant and Rice	134
Zucchini Noodles	135
Quick Chickpea Stew	136
Simple Oven Baked Vegetables	137
Baked Vegetables with Feta Cheese	138
Roasted Asparagus	139
Salads	140
Grilled Chicken Salad	140
Orzo Salad	141
Rice Salad with Feta Cheese	142
Classic Mediterranean Potato Salad	143
Couscous Salad with Feta Cheese	144
Crunchy Broccoli Salad	145
Tuna Salad	146
Baked Shrimp Salad	147
Celery Olive Salad	148
Desserts	149
Grilled Peaches with Yogurt and Honey	149
Fruit Salad	150
Greek Yogurt with Walnuts	151
Greek Yogurt with Strawberries	152
Broiled Figs with Greek Yogurt	153
Fruit Salad with Banana Dressing	154
Greek Yogurt with Cranberries and Nuts	155

7-Day Meal Plan	156
Day 2	156
Day 3	157
Day 4	157
Day 5	158
Day 6	158
Day 7	159

Introduction

When it comes time to worry about your health or lose weight, there are hundreds of diet plans available to choose from. Most promise you that they are the solution you are looking for, but none of them focus on the changes in lifestyle that you need to improve your health. They will focus on the foods you should eat or the ones you should avoid, leaving out the other important aspects.

For those who are worried about their overall health, especially when it comes to their heart health, the Mediterranean diet is the right choice. It contains all the right food choices that you need to keep your body healthy while eliminating foods that are high in cholesterol, cause inflammation, or will lead to more damage throughout your body.

In addition to leading you to the right food choices, the Mediterranean diet will ask you to make some lifestyle changes as well. You can't just eat the right foods and keep your body healthy; you also need to focus on the right amount of exercise, taking time to relax and de-stress, spend time with family and friends, and learn how to improve your overall mood. Once all of these things come together, you are living a healthier life thanks to the Mediterranean lifestyle.

This guidebook is going to take some time to look at the Mediterranean diet and why it may be the right choice for you. This is one of the healthiest diets you will find, with years of clinical research, plus thousands of years of practical use in the Mediterranean area, to prove that it does help with life expectancy, heart health, and many other health conditions. No other diet plan has these kind of results because they don't focus on the whole lifestyle of the participant and don't provide the body with the right nutrition all in one.

If you are ready to take your health in your own hands, the Mediterranean diet is the one diet plan you need to take a look at. It will help you to make the right choices for your life to improve your heart health, even if you've had a heart attack in the past, while making it easier to lose weight, lower your blood pressure, and get your overall health back in line. Take a look through this guidebook and learn how easy it is to add the Mediterranean diet into your life and get the good health you've always dreamed of.

Chapter 1: How Your Diet and Lifestyle are Slowly Killing You

The lifestyle and diet of the typical American is toxic. While many think they are taking good care of their health, most of their food is full of sugars, salt, and fats that are slowly killing us from the inside out. Even the healthier food choices in this country contain preservatives and pesticides that aren't much better than the donuts, fast foods, and covered in salt options that we eat at every chance during the day.

It isn't just the food that Americans choose that are ruining our health as a nation. Most Americans do not take the time to exercise during the day; choosing instead to work jobs that make them sit all day and coming home to just sit on the couch and watch television all night. Add to this the high levels of chronic stress found in most American lives, and it is no wonder that there have been huge rises in the amount of obesity, diabetes, high blood pressure, and heart diseases plaguing us all.

We are told again and again that we need to change our habits to make this condition better. We know that we must get up and exercise and reduce our stress and start eating right, but when surrounded by medications that promise to make it better, surgical procedures that promise to make you skinny and healthy in no time, it is easy to try and take the easy way out.

The American Diet is Toxic

The American diet is one of the unhealthiest diets that you can find. While other cultures work to eat foods that are traditional, are easily found in their countries, and include lots of fresh and good ingredients, the American diet seems to have taken things in a different direction.

Americans love their treats. It is common to go out to eat and get a big meal, one that is often enough to feed two or three people even though they will eat the whole thing themselves. Even if they do intend to cook something at home, it usually includes a meal that can be thrown in the microwave and heated up. Americans will look for any excuse to drink a pop, have some cake, add an extra dessert, and basically eat as much unhealthy food as they possibly can.

Think about the foods you consume on a regular day. You may start out with a heavy breakfast full of pastries, eggs, or sausages in a lot of grease and fat. Others may go for coffee or pick something up on the way to work. Lunch may be something healthy if you remembered to bring it before heading out the door and supper can be hit or miss depending on how many activities go on that night with your family.

Isn't all of this exhausting? Not only are you running around doing all these activities, but you aren't feeding your body the foods it needs to keep up with all this work, causing even more stress on the body. There are three potential times during each busy day that you are going out to eat or picking something that just goes in the microwave. These are not healthy choices and not only are they adding to your waistline, they are also ruining your health.

The typical diet for Americans is not healthy at all. We are more into convenience rather than picking something that is going to refuel the body. In addition, we are so stressed out from work and all the other obligations we have to fit into a day, we can barely fit in a good workout a few times a week much less learn to calm down or even get to sleep at night. All of this is going to add up and start causing big issues with our health.

Short term, this results in exhaustion, irritability, stress, and the inability to really enjoy the day as it comes to us. This may not seem like a big deal at first. We assume that once this big project is over or we get through the holidays, things will slow down and we can finally take care of our health. Unfortunately, this doesn't usually happen and the issues get worse.

The long term problems are the big issue here. While we may feel that we are doing things right and taking care of ourselves, these unhealthy eating habits are slowly draining us and causing us to get sick. Just look at the recent health numbers for Americans; diabetes, obesity, high blood pressure, and heart disease have gone through the roof. Even younger children are facing many of these problems because of our eating choices.

The longer you allow these unhealthy foods, lack of exercise, and high levels of stress to rule your life, the harder it becomes to reverse the damage. You will deal with heart disease, stroke, obesity, and a whole host of other medical issues because you are not taking good care of your body. Unfortunately, by the time you start feeling some of these symptoms, it could already be too late for you to do something.

In order to take back control of your health and start feeling your very best again, you need to make changes to your whole life. It is not enough to just start a few days of exercising each week, although this is a good start. It is not enough to just eat healthy on occasion and hope you get healthier. In fact, you need to combine good eating and good exercise together with healthy ways to manage stress, time spent with friends and family, and a general overhaul of your traditional American lifestyle.

The Mediterranean Diet

If the thought of the traditional American diet makes you feel sick and you are ready to eat something that is healthier for the body, the Mediterranean diet is the right option for you. This diet is better than the American diet because of all the healthier food options, but it doesn't rely on fads like other diets that will only lead to short-term success or will make you sick as well.

The Mediterranean diet is based on the diets of those who live in the Mediterranean area. It has been around for thousands of years and shows the main reason that people in this area are more likely to live longer, have fewer weight-related diseases, and even less heart attack risk. The great news about the Mediterranean diet isn't just that it's effective; you also get many countries' cuisine to follow to help prevent boredom or to mix it up on some days.

One thing to understand about this diet plan though is that it's not all about your diet choices. While other diets simply tell you to eat this and not that, the Mediterranean diet understands that you need to make changes to all aspects of your life if you truly want to get in good health. It isn't enough to just eat the right foods. You will need to work at drinking the right liquids, getting enough quality exercise into your day to take care of the heart, reduce stress, get enough sleep, and so much more. The Mediterranean diet is not just a diet, it is also a lifestyle change.

The Mediterranean diet is one of the best options to help you get back into the healthy lifestyle that you need to keep away many common ailments in the body. For example, the Mediterranean diet has been effective at reducing your risk for:

- Arthritis
- Alzheimer's disease
- Allergies
- Metabolic syndrome
- Diabetes
- High cholesterol
- High blood pressure
- Cancer
- Heart disease
- Depression

But how can the Mediterranean diet promise all of these great health benefits? This is a common question that dieters may ask after trying out many other health plans and never seeing the results. The difference between the Mediterranean diet and some of the other diet plans you may have tried is that the Mediterranean diet is considered synergistic.

Other diet plans are often just going to focus on the foods you eat. They will spend time talking about which nutrients the body needs to stay healthy. And while this is important, it forgets the other aspects of your health that you need to take care of us well. Not only do you need the proper nutrition, but you need the right amount of exercise to keep the body strong, a healthy way to reduce your stress levels, adequate levels of sleep and even time to sit back and relax with friends and family.

The beauty of the Mediterranean diet is that it brings all of these parts together. Yes, you are going to learn about the different foods that are allowed on this diet and which ones you are to skip out on for better health, but it doesn't just focus on the eating. It talks about having dinner with your family, eating foods that are whole and delicious for you, getting outside and exercising, and other ways to reduce your stress and live a fuller and happier life.

When all of these points finally come together, you are getting the best results possible. You are taking care of your mind and body in a way that can help combat many common illnesses and giving yourself a chance for a healthier life.

Chapter 2: The Mediterranean Diet Revealed

The Mediterranean diet has been hailed as one of the best diet plans that you can find. It is all about changing up your lifestyle, not just your diet, in order to become the healthiest version of yourself possible. There are some critics of the Mediterranean diet though. Some think that this diet is too hard to follow, misses out on some of the key nutrients that you need, or that it just doesn't do the things that it promises.

It is important to remember that many of the people who have issues with these diets are the ones who want quick fixes. They want to take a pill to feel better. Or else they are in love with their current plan and aren't interested in changing. Even so, it is still a good idea to go through and learn as much about a particular diet plan before going on it.

Luckily, the Mediterranean diet has had a lot of research done on it over the years. These studies show that the Mediterranean diet is not only effective, it can be even better than some of the most popular diets available. For example, one of the studies that we will discuss below showed that the Mediterranean diet is more effective than the recommendations from the American Heart Association in helping to prevent future heart complications in patients who have had a heart attack.

When it comes to weight control and the health of your heart, the Mediterranean diet is one of the best. This diet is full of non-processed foods that have healthy vitamins and nutrients for the whole body. You will eat foods that come from the earth, ones that are actually made for your body to enjoy, not ones that have ingredients made in a factory. When you combine these foods with a healthier lifestyle, you are going to get tremendous benefits.

Does the Mediterranean Diet Work?

Unlike many popular diet programs available today, the Mediterranean diet has been studied extensively. The landmark study was published in the New England Journal of Medicine (February 27, 2014) compared a low fat diet t the Mediterranean diet. This study was stopped after just 4.8 years thanks to the great results that were found. In fact, those who followed the Mediterranean diet found a 30 percent reduction in most major cardiovascular events. After reviewing this study, health experts stated that the Mediterranean diet proves as effective as drugs when helping prevent and reduce the risk of cardiovascular disease.

http://www.nejm.org/doi/full/10.1056/NEJMx140004

This is just one of the many studies done on the Mediterranean diet so far which show how wonderful this diet can be to your overall health! Some of the other studies include:

The Seven Countries Study

This study spanned twenty years and was led by Dr. Ancel Keys. It began in the late 1950s and followed 13000 men, all from different countries, including Japan, United States, Finland, Netherlands, Yugoslavia, Greece, and Italy to see if a diet that was low in processed foods and saturated fat had a lower rate of death from heart disease. Dr. Keys found that those who lived in the Mediterranean area had the lowest heart disease rates of anyone. In fact, those in this area had a 90% lower likelihood of dying from heart attacks compared to men in America.

http://www.sevencountriesstudy.com/

The Lyon Diet Heart Study

In this study, the Mediterranean diet was compared to the diet similar to what the American Heart Association recommends to heart attack survivors. During the study, it was found that the Mediterranean diet provided more protection against heart attacks. In fact, the Mediterranean diet was able to decrease the risk of more cardiac events by 73 percent and the risk of death by 70 percent.

http://circ.ahajournals.org/content/103/13/1823.full

The DART Study

The DART Study took a look at over 2000 men who had heart attacks before. It was testing the hypothesis that the fatty acids found in fish like tuna and salmon, are able to protect against heart disease. The results were that taking in a modest amount of fatty fish a few times a week, usually about 300 grams each week, can reduce your risk of dying from heart disease by 32 percent.

http://thedartstudy.com/

The Singh Indo-Mediterranean Diet Study

In this study, 499 patients who were at a high risk factor for heart disease were placed on a Mediterranean style diet full of almonds, walnuts, whole grains, vegetables, and fruits. During the time of this study it was found that this diet resulted in a reduction in cholesterol in the bloodstream and was associated with a reduction in heart attacks. The subjects were also found to have fewer heart related issues compared to those on a traditional diet.

http://www.medscape.com/viewarticle/785895

The Alzheimer's Disease Study

This study was done by Dr. Nikolaos Scarmeas and others from the Columbia University Medical Center. This study demonstrated that not only did the Mediterranean diet help with heart disease, it helped to reduce the risk of patients developing Alzheimer's disease by a full 68 percent. Another study that this same group performed showed that patients who had Alzheimer's disease, and who were placed on the Mediterranean diet, had a reduced rate of mortality.

https://www.ncbi.nlm.nih.gov/pubmed/23680940

The Metabolic Syndrome Study

This study was performed by Dr. Katherine Esposito and colleagues to see the effects of the Mediterranean diet on metabolic syndrome which included symptoms like high cholesterol, elevated blood pressure, high blood sugars, and obesity. It was found that the Mediterranean diet was able to improve all of the symptoms of metabolic syndrome.

http://www.medscape.com/viewarticle/833218

These are just a few of the studies that show how great the Mediterranean diet can be for your health. Studies have linked the trans fat and saturated fat found in the Western diet to a higher risk of heart disease, as well as other diseases. But in the Mediterranean diet, you are limiting your saturated fat intake and trans fats are almost non-existent. This is a huge contrast from the typical diet that most Americans enjoy and can be the major influence on whether you develop many life-threatening diseases.

Others feel that the foods in this diet help to decrease inflammation. Inflammation has long played a role in the development of diabetes, cancer, heart disease and more. When you consume foods that decrease inflammation, you can help to prevent some of these common diseases in your own body.

No matter the reason, many studies have proven that the Mediterranean diet is the best choice when it comes to the health of your heart as well as protecting you from a whole host of other diseases.

Chapter 3: Unlock the Mediterranean Lifestyle

The Mediterranean diet is a unique diet that is quite a bit different than what most Americans enjoy, but is one that has been around for thousands of years. It is based of the diet and lifestyle choices of those who live in the Mediterranean area.

There are so many benefits of choosing this area to emulate. First, the people of this area have the best longevity out of anywhere else in the world. Their healthy diet and lifestyle allows them to avoid sudden death, especially from heart-related conditions, as well as protects them from many diseases that are common in America today.

In addition, the Mediterranean area contains many different countries from Greece to France, Italy to Spain and much more. This provides you with a lot of variety when it comes to picking the recipes and meals that you enjoy. Unlike some of the other diet plans you may encounter, most of which are not that effective for weight loss and overall health, the Mediterranean diet allows you to make a lot of choices and have some variety to prevent boredom in meal choices.

The studies have shown how effective the Mediterranean diet can be for your whole health. Whether you are concentrating on your heart health, preventing Alzheimer's, reducing inflammation, or working on your waistline, the Mediterranean diet has proven itself again and again.

But this diet plan is more than just the foods you eat. While it is important to eat foods full of the nutrients your body needs to stay healthy, there is so much more to it than just what you eat. You need to also learn how to reduce your stress levels, enjoy life, get in enough exercise, and make your whole lifestyle, not just your meal choices, healthier.

This chapter will focus more on the lifestyle choices that you need to make when choosing the Mediterranean diet to improve your health.

The Foods of the Mediterranean Diet

Understanding the main components of the Mediterranean diet is crucial if you want to see the great heart and health benefits promised with this diet plan. Let's take a look at some of these components and how each one will be beneficial to your health.

Whole Grains

Whole grains, ones that have not been refined before selling, are a big part of the Mediterranean diet. The whole grain kernel contains three layers that have the fiber, protein, and vitamins and minerals that you need to get all the nutrition out of your bread products. When you refine your grains, like many of the options in the American diet, you are getting rid of two of these layers, effectively getting rid of the phytochemicals, vitamins, and fiber that are so get in whole grains.

Always make sure that you are picking out whole grains at all times. Some of the whole grains found on the Mediterranean diet include barley, quinoa, kasha, and oatmeal.

Fresh Produce

The main cornerstone of the Mediterranean diet is fresh produce. Go anywhere in the Mediterranean basin and you will find markets full of fresh fruits and vegetables. These produce include fiber, minerals, vitamins, and complex carbs that can do wonders for reducing cancer and heart disease. The phytonutrients found in the skin of produce are the best for improving your health.

When it comes to fresh produce, make sure to get a wide variety. This helps you to get more nutrients in your meals rather than the same ones each day. Think about adding yellow squash, spinach, red apples, blueberries, cherries, oranges, and other great options to get all the nutritional benefits you're looking for.

There are several places you can go to find the best produce. Farmer's markets are a good idea or consider growing some in your backyard to ensure they are fresh. Buying at the grocery store works as well but you will need to keep in mind that the further the produce had to travel, the fewer nutrients are inside. If you live far away from the origin of your produce and it is winter, you may want to consider going with frozen fruit to get your nutrients.

Nuts

Nuts are an important part of the Mediterranean diet. Walnuts and almonds are great for adding in some of the omega-3 fatty acids your body needs to prevent heart disease as well as plenty of vitamins, fiber, and protein. These are the perfect snack when taken in moderation, to help keep you full and happy until the next meal. Several studies have also found that eating nuts on a regular basis can help with heart disease, while lowering your cholesterol levels.

Legumes and Beans

The Mediterranean diet also encourages eating legumes and beans as they are a good source of fiber and will help to reduce your cholesterol levels while curbing the appetite. They also have a lot of good vitamins and protein inside and work good as a base to some of your favorite dishes.

Fish

Oily fish is found in high concentration in the Mediterranean area and is full of healthy omega-3 fatty acids and protein. In fact, this is one of the best sources of protein that you can eat on this diet. Omega-3's are great for lowering your triglyceride levels and cholesterol to keep your heart happy while also helping to reduce inflammation in the body. The Mediterranean diet recommends that you eat fish at least a few times each week to get adequate amounts of this nutrient and choose options like Pollock, flounder, trout, sardines, tuna, and salmon.

Olive Oil

When it comes to cooking oils, nothing is better than olive oil. This is a good substitute to margarine or butter while still providing all the flavor that you are looking for in your foods. A study from Boston showed that having a diet high in nuts and olive oil can help you to sustain your weight loss over time compared to using a low fat diet. The olive oil can also help to increase the HDL cholesterol, or the good cholesterol, while decreasing the LDL, or bad cholesterol, in your bloodstream, helping to protect your heart.

Red Wine

Red wine is allowed in moderation on this diet plan. Red wine has several advantages to your health thanks to the resveratrol and polyphenols that help to promote the health of your heart. It is also good for helping raise the good cholesterol while lowering the bad cholesterol to keep your heart healthy. Keep in mind that this is not a license to drink as much red wine as you want. One glass for women and up to two for men a day as a maximum to promote your health without overdoing it.

If you are not accustomed to drinking red wine, or other alcoholic beverages, it is usually recommended that you don't start just because you are on this diet plan. You can get many of the same benefits from regular grape juice, as long as you pick a type that has no added sugars or preservatives in it. If you already enjoy an alcoholic beverage on occasion, switching it over to wine can be the best choice.

The Foods That Ruin Your Health

There are a number of foods that you will need to avoid while following the Mediterranean diet. Many of these are popular options in the American diet, but they are slowly raising your cholesterol levels, causing inflammation, and doing other things that are detrimental to your health. Some of the things that you should avoid when it comes to the Mediterranean lifestyle include:

- Red meat—keep this limited. It is recommended to have red meats just a few times a month to avoid adding more cholesterol or saturated fat to your diet.

- Sugars—the sugars you consume should come from fruits and vegetables, not from baked goods and other unhealthy foods.
- Butter and margarine—if you want to flavor your foods, use olive oil instead since this has extra nutrients that are so good for the body.
- Processed grains—these take out all of the good nutrients from the grains and makes them unhealthy and not filling.
- Too much alcohol—too much alcohol can be dangerous to your health. While a bit of red wine is allowed, you need to be careful with drinking too much or other forms of alcohol.
- Milk—one of the most surprising changes found in the Mediterranean diet is that milk is not encouraged. Milk can be contributed to many common health conditions and if you drink the recommended three glasses a day, you are adding an extra 450 calories into the diet. If you must drink milk for your diet, make sure that you go with low fat options.
- Canned produce—while it may look like the same fruits and vegetables you enjoy and it may be less expensive at the store, canned produce is so bad for your health. All of the nutrition has been taken out of those products and since most are placed in a sugary juice to keep safe until you open, they are not that healthy. Avoid these and go with either fresh or frozen produce for this diet plan.
- Canned goods—anything that is canned is a bad idea on the Mediterranean diet. This diet plan encourages eating healthy and whole foods and most things in cans are full of sugars, salt, and other preservatives that are hard on the body. Learn how to make things homemade rather than purchasing them in a can.
- Salt—salt can be really hard on your heart, especially when taken in such high amounts as found in the American diet. Salt products are often discouraged on this diet because they can raise blood pressure and make the heart work harder than it needs to. While a bit is fine in moderation, many types of foods come with salt already in them so it is best to just avoid adding salt to anything to stay within your daily recommendations.

For some people, kicking all the bad habits out at once can make the diet seem almost unbearable. You may want to consider going slowly. You could start by adding in all the healthy parts of this diet plan and then slowly kick one or two bad habits out every week or so. Over time, you will eventually have gotten rid of all your bad habits and will be completely on the diet portion of the Mediterranean diet.

Other Aspects of the Mediterranean Diet

Your food choices are not the only important decisions on the Mediterranean diet. In fact, you are going to see very little in terms of results if you don't add in the other aspects, such as relaxation, daily exercise, stress reduction, and even smoking cessation to your daily routine. Let's take a look at some of the lifestyle changes that you must make to really enjoy all the benefits of the Mediterranean diet.

Stress Reduction

Those who live in the Western world are plagued by stress on a daily basis. They have to worry about their jobs, always be available, have a million activities, and can't seem to keep up. Those who live in the Mediterranean countries though tend to have less stress. They are able to enjoy their meals with friends and family rather than always being on the run. They get time to relax with their meals, sometimes even taking short naps after lunch; a little nap in the middle of the day is also beneficial as it can reduce your risk of dying from heart disease by 37 percent!

Having a bit of stress in your life is not necessarily a bad thing. It can help you to stay motivated to get things done and in some cases can help you stay alive. But the issue in America is chronic stress. This is when the stress is around you all the time. The hectic lifestyle of the average American can make you feel like you are always on the run and ready to fight or flight at a moment's notice.

This chronic stress is bad on your health in so many ways. First, the stress hormones, adrenaline and cortisol, are going to increase which can mess with your blood pressure and may form blood clots. In fact, there have been numerous studies that show how chronic stress can increase your risk of heart attack. It can also make you overeat, adding to obesity and other health related issues, irritable to others, and even depression.

Luckily, there are different steps you can take to help combat the stress you are feeling. Some of the best steps for stress reduction include:

- Meditation
- Exercising daily
- Taking time to smile and laugh each day
- Learning how to have a positive outlook on your life

- Yoga
- Do something that you enjoy at least once a week
- Live within your means rather than keeping up with the Jones's
- Set goals that will push you but are realistic in your life
- Have meaningful relationships with your friends and family
- Praying

Meditation and exercise are probably the two best ways to reduce stress, although the others can certainly help. Meditation is a great way to get away from the world, even for just ten or fifteen minutes, and just concentrate on your good energy and relax. You should take one or two sessions each day to calm the mind, get away from the things that stress you out, and then come back refreshed and as good as new. This, coupled with a good exercise program, can ensure that your mind is relaxed and ready to take on the new day.

Exercise

Another aspect of the Mediterranean diet is to exercise each day. It can be a great way to help you manage stress, but it will also help to keep your bones strong, lower your blood pressure, raise good cholesterol, and helps you to feel a sense of well-being. Exercise can help you to improve lung function, bring about muscle tone, increase your metabolism, and reduce fatigue.

Many Americans live sedentary lives. They will spend all day at work sitting in a chair and then barely get up once they get home. This plus their poor eating habits are leading them to weigh more and have many more health issues. And it isn't just something that people out of weight should worry about. Being fit, even if you are overweight, is much better on your health than being skinny and never working out.

Sometimes it is hard to find time to get all that exercising done throughout the day. It is important to attempt 30 minutes or more of exercise each day, but incorporating exercise into your daily activities can make this easier and keeps your body up and moving.

Some of the things that you can do to help get more exercise into your day and keep your body running well include:

- Walk for 30 minutes each day. You do not need to go outside or even have a treadmill to do this. March in place and turn on your favorite television show. You would be amazed at how quickly time goes by and how you can still do something enjoyable at the same time.
- Park further away at the store. Even if it is just a few spots further away, it can add up.
- Use the stairs. It is always better to use the stairs rather than relying on the elevator. If you are on the top floor, consider doing half the distance in stairs and half in the elevator until you build up endurance.
- Walk before lunch. If you have an hour lunch break, take a 15- or 20-minute walk before you eat.
- Get a pedometer. You should strive to get 10,000 steps into each day and a pedometer can be a great motivator to get you there.

It is a good idea to mix up your workouts to get the best benefits. Cardio is great for the heart and can build up endurance and so much more. Try to find a good activity that you enjoy, such as swimming, dancing, biking, running, or walking, and do this as a workout three or four times a week for 30 minutes or more each time.

Other forms of exercise are important as well. Strength training can really work those muscles and will speed up your metabolism more than anything else. You can incorporate this into your routine a few times a week, starting out slowly and building up to heavier weight.

And don't forget some of that nice stretching. This gives the body a bit of a break and allows you to lengthen out the body, reduces strains and other injuries, and can even relax the body. Consider some Pilates, which mixes strength training and stretches together, or yoga to calm down the mind and body.

Sleep

As someone who is working on improving their overall health, it is important to get enough sleep into your day. You could be doing everything else perfectly right, but if you are not getting enough sleep, you are not going to see good health results. Most Americans are woefully short on the amount of sleep they need. They are lucky to get six hours of sleep each night and naps are non-existent.

Lack of sufficient amounts of sleep can have huge effects on all aspects of your health and can make all the other good lifestyle changes you are working on ineffective. Some of the health benefits that you may be dealing with if you don't get enough sleep include:

- Impaired brain activity
- Moodiness
- Depression
- Weight gain
- Memory issues
- Depression
- Illness
- Heart disease
- High blood pressure
- Type 2 diabetes

The best thing that you can do is strive to get eight to nine hours of sleep each day, even if you need to take a nap during the day to reach this number. Creating a quite atmosphere around you before falling asleep, getting into a routine, turning the computer and phone of at least an hour before bed, not eating too close to bed time, and other activities can make it easier than ever to get the sleep that you need to stay healthy.

The Commandments of the Mediterranean Diet

If you want to see the most success with the Mediterranean diet, you need to follow these simple commandments:

1. Always have a sense of humor. It is important to laugh, smile and have fun in life.
2. Relax. This is really important after your meals, but take time to sit back and relax as much as you can during the day.
3. Exercise each day. It is best to get at least 30 minutes of exercise each day.
4. Drink alcohol in moderation. Red wine is the best but keep this to one or two glasses maximum each day.

5. Do not smoke as this can bring about a myriad of health issues later on.
6. Drink plenty of water to keep hydrated.
7. Watch your portion sizes. While there are many great foods on this diet plan, you do need to be careful about how much you consume.
8. Avoid the butter and margarine and instead go for olive oil or other suitable spreads.
9. Eat a large variety of foods. You should be going for foods that are fresh and non-processed for good results.
10. Avoid excess sodium, refined sugar, trans fat, and saturated fats.

And that is it! The Mediterranean diet is all about a lifestyle change, rather than just a meal planning change, but it does not have to be complicated. Simply taking care of your body and feeding it with the energy and nutrition that it needs, rather than the processed and junk food most Americans enjoy, can make a big difference on your levels of health.

Chapter 4: Is the Mediterranean Diet Right for Me?

With all the diet plans on the market, it is hard to hear through the chatter and find the one that is right for you. So many of them promise to be the perfect choice or weight loss and perfect health, but they give contradictory advice. For example, some say that you need to limit fats and proteins while others blame carbs for your bad health. They are completely opposite, so which one is in the right? While some diet plans are dangerous and bad for your health, sometimes it is hard to tell which ones are a bad idea right from the start.

First off, if you ever run across a diet that promises to be a quick fix, run the other way. These often have no scientific basis behind them and can make you sick really quick. Even if you don't get sick on the diet, you will find that the results are temporary and too hard to keep up for a long time; once you go off the diet, your poor health and weight will all come back.

Let's take a look at some of the most popular diet plans out there and determine why they may not be the best for your health.

Low Fat Diets

These diets have been around for years now and are concentrating on eating a high carbohydrate and low fat diet. Many of them will rely on vegetarian meals because many meats are too high in fat for them. They are really hard to follow and most Americans will find them boring or too difficult to keep up with. Even if you are able to keep up with this diet, you may be missing out on some of the heathier fats that your body needs to function.

The point with these diets is to get rid of all the fats you consume. It misses out on the important fact that you need some fats to stay healthy and that there are two different categories of fats that you have to be aware of. The good fats help you with energy and proper functioning of your heart while the other fats will make you sick. The Mediterranean diet can help you to understand the difference while still getting in all the good fats your body needs.

The American Heart Association Diet

This is a diet plan that many heart attack patients will choose. They assume that it is best for their health and will help them to prevent future heart issues. This is another low fat diet that has actually been proven to decrease the good cholesterol in your body, allowing for more heart disease to progress despite your best efforts.

The biggest issue with the AHA diet is that it contains less omega-3 fat and monounsaturated fat compared to the Mediterranean diet which means it could lead to a higher risk of developing heart attacks and other heart diseases over time. In fact, the Lyon Heart Study showed that those who followed the Mediterranean diet had a reduction of 73 percent in heart attack or death compared to those who followed the AHA diet.

Low Carb Diets

This would include diets like the Atkins or South Beach diet. These are relatively new so there isn't much in terms of the long term effects of following these diets. Many doctors are worried that these diets would cause more of a risk of cancer and heart disease in the long term. You will find that these diets rely more on fats, which isn't necessarily a bad thing, but many followers don't stick with the regimen and eat foods with saturated fats and cholesterol since they technically fit into the description, raising their heart attack risks.

The biggest issue with this is that they do cause rapid weight loss to occur right in the beginning so many people want to jump on and see their own results. But most of these weight loss events can come from water loss and this change in fluids in the body can cause kidney malfunctions and cardiac arrhythmias.

They also rely on eating more saturated fats while reducing the amount of carbs that you consume, and many longer term followers will see a rise in their LDL cholesterol. Overall, these diets add in too much of the bad fats, are hard to maintain, and will eventually lead the person to go back to their old habits rather than see better health.

There are a number of bad side effects that come with low carb diets and these can be magnified quite a bit because the carbs are not there to help counteract the effects at all. Some of the increased health risks of using the low carb diets include:

- Optic neuropathy
- Kidney malfunctions including kidney stones
- Impaired memory
- Halitosis or bad breath
- Elevated cholesterol
- Gout
- Elevated CRP which is an indicator of inflammation
- Diabetes
- Deficiency of important micronutrients
- Diabetes
- Coronary heart disease
- Cardia arrhythmia
- Cancer

Most doctors will not recommend these diets to their patients. These low carb diets are hard on the body, make it hard for you to get some of the nutrients that the body needs, and can make you really sick. It is best to choose a healthier diet, such as the Mediterranean diet, to help you get in the best health possible without complications.

Why Should I Choose the Mediterranean Diet?

Unlike many of the other diets mentioned above, the Mediterranean is a balanced diet that includes all of the healthy nutrients that you need, including complex carbs and healthy fats. It is one of the best options to use when trying to lose weight while also maintaining your health. Just think about it, what other diet has been continually in use for thousands of years? Not only will you be able to lose weight though, but also when you combine this diet with lowering your stress and increasing your exercise, you will be able to improve so many aspects of your health including your blood pressure, blood sugar, cholesterol, and heart health.

Secrets to Losing Weight

There is no secret to losing weight. You simply need to burn more calories than you are consuming. Most Americans are taking in way more calories than they need, especially if they spend most of the day sitting around. Americans are known for large meals, snacking, and just not moving around much. All of these extra calories and the sedentary lifestyle that accompanies will easily explain why obesity is such a problem in this country.

So first you need to learn how to eat smart. Limiting the portion sizes of our food is a good place to start. Most of our prepackaged foods come in portions way too big for us to eat in one sitting. Even making food in your home can lead to oversized portions if you don't know what to look for. While a scale can help to measure out food, you can learn a few ways to eyeball your portion sizes. For example, a three ounce portion of meat will be the same thickness as a deck of cards and a medium sized fruit will be like a tennis ball.

Next, you can burn more calories when you are more active in your day. You can only cut so many calories out of your meals without starving yourself, but you can add more activity into the day. You can walk around more, start an exercise routine, and learn other ways to keep up and moving.

And third, you need to cut out all the bad foods in your diet. You need to avoid the saturated fats, trans fats, refined sugars, processed foods, and all those other things that are bad for your health. The Mediterranean diet will help you do this.

The Mediterranean diet is one of the most effective at helping you to lose weight. This is because on the Mediterranean diet:

- Exercise is important and should be included in your daily life.
- Food portions are accurate, rather than super sized like on the American diet. This allows you to get the right servings to stay healthy without all the extras.
- Consuming foods that are high in fiber like what is required on this diet allows you to feel full while eating fewer calories.

- Consuming complex carbs can help you to feel fuller, eat fewer calories, and can keep obesity away.
- Trans fats, which are known for obesity and weight gain, are avoided on the Mediterranean diet while the healthier fats are highly encouraged. You don't have to avoid fats altogether, you just need to learn which ones are the best for your health.

Lowering Your Cholesterol

Not only will you be able to lose weight with the Mediterranean diet, you can also lower your cholesterol in a healthy and natural way. Studies have shown that this diet plan is able to lower the LDL, or bad, cholesterol, while raising the HDL, or good, cholesterol all while lowering your triglycerides. In fact, some patients were able to eliminate or reduce the use of cholesterol medications after a short time on the Mediterranean diet because it is so effective in the body.

There are a number of foods recommended on the Mediterranean diet that are especially good at impacting your cholesterol including:

- Red wine
- Cinnamon
- Soy protein
- Coldwater fish
- Beans
- Nuts
- Soy protein
- Fruits and vegetable
- Olive oil
- Whole grains

These foods are able to interfere with how your body absorbs cholesterol, making it easier to just pass it through the body rather than absorbing it into the blood vessels. In addition to the foods you eat, the exercise recommended on the Mediterranean diet will help with lowering the bad cholesterol in your arteries as well.

Lowering Your Blood Pressure

High blood pressure can be detrimental to your health. Blood pressure is basically the force that your blood makes against the artery walls. There are two numbers used to determine your blood pressure; systolic is the level of force when the heart is beating and the diastolic pressure is the force as the heart relaxes. Both of these are important to determining the health of the heart. If you have high blood pressure and don't treat it, you could end up with many health issues including a higher risk of heart attack, vascular disease, kidney disease, and more.

Many things are going to influence your blood pressure. The foods you eat, especially ones that are high in cholesterol and sodium, can make your blood pressure soar. High levels of chronic stress have been linked to an elevated blood pressure and can have the same harmful effects on your body as a poor diet. Lack of sleep, lack of exercise, and genetics all play a role in how high your blood pressure is.

Regardless of the reason you are dealing with high blood pressure, it is important to get it down as quickly as possible. The Mediterranean diet is able to help in many ways. First, it will work to eliminate all the foods that are causing your high blood pressure and replace them with ones that are healthier and will keep the blood pressure, and your heart, in good working order.

In addition, the Mediterranean diet is all about changing your lifestyle to be healthier. Since you will add more exercise and learn healthy ways to reduce your stress levels, you will be hitting your blood pressure in several ways. When the stress reduction, better nutrition, and exercise come together, it is easier to reduce your high blood pressure in a natural way without medications.

Nutrition

No other diet allows for the great nutrition that you will find from the Mediterranean diet. Many diets take out whole food groups in the hopes that you will forgo some of the bad stuff that your body doesn't need. But since you are missing out on important nutrients, and perhaps taking in more of another bad nutrient that your body doesn't need as well.

But the Mediterranean diet doesn't cut out whole food groups. It recognizes that you need the good carbs, the produce, the protein and the good fats all in one. You will just need to get rid of a few foods that are bad on the body, rather than getting rid of a whole food group. This allows you to get rid of the bad while keeping all of the good that your body needs.

The foods on the Mediterranean diet will provide your body with everything that it needs, as long as you remember to include a wide variety of different options. You are not going to provide your body with all the nutrients it needs if you just eat apples every day for your fruit or the same kind of fish on every meal. Mix it up with a lot of variety in your meals and you will get the best nutrition and health that your body needs.

Exercise

Exercise is an important part of following this diet plan. Most Americans spend too little time exercising each day. Exercise is so important to your health. It helps to lower your blood pressure, assists in weight loss, improves your mood, and can help you to strengthen the heart and keep it stronger. The Mediterranean diet is one of the few diet plans that expressly encourages exercise to get the results that you want. Find a healthy way for you to get in some exercise each day to receive all these great benefits.

Stress Management

The Mediterranean diet recognizes that the level of stress you deal with will directly influence your health. Those who are under a lot of stress will have trouble with overeating, high blood pressure, low levels of energy, heart conditions, and so much more. The longer these conditions are around in the body, the harder it is to take care of the problems.

Learning how to handle your stress is one of the best ways to live a healthy life. This is why the Mediterranean diet focuses so much on this. You should consider taking time to relax and do things that you enjoy each day. Try some yoga or light stretching, learn to say no when you have too much going on at work, take a vacation, read, get more sleep at night, and do other things that help you de-stress and really enjoy life.

Smoking Cessation

Smoking is hard on your health, especially when it comes to your heart health. Nicotine in cigarettes will cause the arteries to constrict and the carbon monoxide will cause less oxygenated blood to get to the heart muscle. Even one cigarette a day can cause these issues and make you really sick, regardless of how many other healthy choices you make in your life.

The Mediterranean diet encourages you to stop smoking right away. There are quite a few methods available to help you stop smoking including hypnosis, acupuncture, or nicotine gum and patches. You can also discuss this with your doctor if the other methods aren't working as well for you. It is important to stop as soon as possible to ensure that you get your health back on track.

The Mediterranean diet is a lifestyle change. It requires you to make changes in more than just your meal choices so that you can really work on your overall health. You will work on increasing your exercise, work on reducing your stress, and eating foods that help to lower your weight, blood pressure, and so much more. No other diet plan on the market can make these promises for overall good health and still be sustainable for your whole life. When you need to get your health on track right away or you are ready to take preventative action to stay healthy, the Mediterranean diet is the right one for you.

Chapter 5: The Mediterranean Diet Essentials

We have spent a lot of time talking about the components of the Mediterranean diet and how you are going to need to change some important aspects of your eating as well as your lifestyle to finally get your health back in line. But why are all these components so important? Why do you need to take in certain fats and avoid the others? Why is a traditional American diet so bad for the body while the Mediterranean diet, which goes against many popular diets, is so effective for your health? This chapter will take a look at some of the main components of this diet plan to help you understand how the pieces come together.

What You Need to Know About Fats

Fats have gotten a bad name in our society. Many assume that all fats are bad. They will try to get as few fats into their diet as possible when losing weight, assuming these are evil and are making them hold onto the pounds. The problem here is that you do need fats. Fats are important to many parts of the body functioning properly and without them, you will lose out on energy and start to have more health issues.

The trick here is to recognize the difference between the good fats that help you have energy and stay healthy, and the bad fats that are adding on the pounds and making you sick. For example, healthy fats like omega-3s can be good for your brain health and can reduce the risk of heart disease. On the other hand, saturated fats like those found at a fast food restaurant can lead you to stroke, heart disease, diabetes, and more.

The Good

First, let's take a look at the good fats. These would include monounsaturated and polyunsaturated fats. Omega-6 and Omega-3 fatty acids will fall into the polyunsaturated fat category so make sure that you are eating these on the diet as well. These are great for helping to improve your cholesterol levels, improve brain functioning, reduce stroke and other heart diseases, and decrease inflammation. There are a variety of options that you can go for to get these healthy fats including nuts, seeds, vegetables, oily fish, and some vegetable oils.

The Bad

On the other side of things, there are some fats that are bad for you. These are the ones that are going to raise your risk of cancer and heart disease all while raising your LDL cholesterol. These are the ones that most diet plans mean for you to avoid, but which get placed in the same category with the good fats and can make you avoid all fats. But in reality, you just need to avoid certain kinds of fats, mostly the saturated fats.

These fats are the ones that are commonly found in the American diet. They are found in lard, cheese, milk, butter, and red meat as well as palm and coconut oils. They are also found in abundance when it comes to eating out, freezer foods, baked goods, and other things that may taste amazing, but are messing with your health.

Now, the Mediterranean diet does not ask you to completely get rid of these food sources. A bit of saturated fat can be used properly in the body to help out with energy and you are allowed to have small amounts of red meat and milk products on this diet plan. The issue comes when we eat these foods in abundance and start to have too much saturated fat in our bloodstream. This leads to elevated heart disease risks, on top of other health concerns. If you choose to consume the bad fats, keep it to a minimum; usually a few times a month is all that is recommended.

The Ugly

While saturated fats are really bad for the body, they are still allowed in extreme moderation with this diet plan. But trans fats are the worst of the worst when it comes to your health. They are known to raise the bad cholesterol, lower your good cholesterol, increase your risk of blood clots, and increase inflammation all throughout the body. Because of all these negative side effects, trans fats have been linked numerous times with diabetes, cancer, and heart disease.

There are many places that you can find trans fats in the American diet including frozen foods, baked goods, crackers, cookies, French fries, margarine, and potato chips. These aren't natural fats; instead they are ones that are manufactured so that your favorite foods are able to last for a longer time on the shelves.

The American diet includes way too many of the bad fats without enough of the good fats. This results in us putting more calories, cholesterol, and other bad things into our bodies without getting enough of the good fats that we need to stay healthy and strong. It is important to make these changes as soon as possible to see the best results.

Learning how to take these out of the diet and replace them with other healthier options is key. For example, creating your own French fries at home with potatoes, or better yet with sweet potatoes, can give you that craving without all the bad fats. Vegetables can be cooked in the oven to give that crispy taste of potato chips without all the bad stuff. Slowly you can eliminate some of the trans fats, along with the saturated fats, to improve your health.

Understanding Omega-3 and Omega-6 Fatty Acids

Many Americans don't get the amount of omega-3s that they need to stay healthy. This is because we aren't eating the foods that have omega-3s inside. For example, fish, vegetables, free range cattle, and fruits are all good sources of omega-3s that were enjoyed up until the beginning of the Industrial Revolution. We grew our own foods and ate things that were all natural and good for the body.

But once the Industrial Revolution started, we were looking more for convenience rather than what was good for us. Prepacked foods, those with long shelf lives, fast foods, and more became the norm and we started to slowly edge out how many omega-3s we desperately need.

When it comes to the American diet, we may have cut out the healthy omega-3s that we need, but we are increasing the amount of omega-6 in our diet. They come from many of our protein sources, oils, and more. Now, eating omega-6s are important for our health and we can't just ignore them and not take any in. They work with omega-3 to keep the brain and body functioning properly, but they need to have the right ratio together to see the results. When one becomes too prevalent, especially when that one is omega-6, it can be detrimental to your health.

The ratio of omega-6 and omega-3 is really important for helping us maintain our health. For example, omega-6 encourages inflammation while omega-3 will cause inflammation to go away so the omega-3s are important for counteracting some of the other nutrients in your body to keep away pain and other issues. In the traditional American diet, omega-6 is consumed in huge proportions because it is found so easily. Many Americans will have a ration of omega-6 to omega-3 somewhere between 10/1 to 20/1 when it should be 1/1. This imbalance will cause issues like:

- Asthma
- Arthritis
- Allergies
- Acne
- Inflammatory bowel disease
- Hypertension
- Sudden cardiac death
- Heart disease
- Cancer
- Diabetes
- Depression
- Disorder of the heart rhythm

The great thing about the Mediterranean diet is that it works to alter this ratio so it is back in line. It helps you to pick foods that will keep the omega-3s and the omega-6s in the perfect ratio.

The Lowdown on Carbs

There are two main thoughts when it comes to carbs in most modern diets; they either love carbs or they forbid them completely. Carbs are a big source of nutrition and energy and can help you get through the day. But just like fats, there are two types of carbs you can choose.

Simple carbs, such as candy, baked goods, and soda, are basically sugars. Once they get into the body, they will be converted into sugar and can make your blood sugar and insulin levels go all over the place when you eat too much. While it may be fine to eat these as a treat on occasion, eating them all the time will result in diabetes and other health conditions.

The carbs that you should concentrate on are the complex carbs. These are options like fruits and vegetables, cereal, oatmeal, and whole grain breads. These are longer strands of carbs that will take longer to metabolize and break down. You will have energy to last a long time and won't have the big spikes in your blood sugar levels like you do with simple foods. They will fill you up, curb your appetite, and often provide many more nutrients than you find with simple carbs.

On the Mediterranean diet, complex carbs are highly encouraged with each meal. Fruits and vegetables have a lot of the complex carbs that you will need throughout the day, but eating whole grain pasta, breads, and other options can be great for your health as well.

What to Drink on the Mediterranean Diet?

What you drink on this diet plan is important too. There are so many options of beverages in the American diet, and many of them are full of added fats, sugars, preservatives, and other things that your body just doesn't need. For example, those coffees from Starbucks are probably not the healthiest option you can choose when it comes to quenching your thirst due to the sugars, flavorings, and other additions.

The first thing that you should focus on drinking is plenty of water. It is recommended that you take in at least eight glasses of water when on this diet plan. This helps you to stay hydrated throughout the day and can prevent higher blood pressure, blood clots, and more. If you workout often or live in a tropical area, make sure to drink more water.

Sometimes juices can be a nice addition to this diet. This does not mean that you should go out and drink ten glasses of this each day, but having a glass of whole fruit juice, the kind without a lot of added sugar, can ensure that you are getting some more vitamins and antioxidants into your day. Keep in mind that if you have a choice, the whole fruit is better than fruit juice in terms of nutrients for your body.

Next on the list is coffee and tea. Caffeine is generally avoided on this diet plan because it can cause dehydration and other issues with your nervous system. But most people on this diet plan are in the habit of drinking one or two cups of coffee each day. Just make sure to avoid the blended drinks since they take away all the good stuff from coffee. Adding tea to your diet, especially green tea is a great idea. The health antioxidants are great for helping to lower bad cholesterol, prevent blood clot formation, and prevents cancer cells from growing. Consider having some green tea in the afternoon to help your heart.

Alcoholic beverages should be avoided for the most part on this diet plan. While red wine can have many antioxidants that are good for the whole body, beer, whiskey and other options are really bad for your heart. You are probably fine having a bit on occasion, usually no more than one serving in a day, but you will want to be careful about consuming too much or you can make yourself sick and cause more heart conditions than you were dealing with in the beginning.

The Milk Question

Most diet plans recommend that you have three or more servings of milk products each day. This is a huge myth in American dieting that can really harm your health. First off, going with three glasses of milk each day will add 15 grams of saturated fat and 450 calories to your diet without giving you all that much nutrition. Add in the hormones that many cows are given to produce more milk and the antibiotics that have later been found in the blood samples of those who drink milk, and milk is not the best option for you.

If you are someone who drinks milk on a regular basis, you may have an increase in a variety of health issues including:

- Prostate cancer
- Ovarian cancer
- Multiple sclerosis
- Heart disease
- GI disturbances
- Diabetes

It is best to avoid milk as much as possible when following the Mediterranean diet, but if you are a big fan or can't give up milk, you should go with almond milk or fat free milk in moderation. This is the same advice you should heed for any kind of milk products including yogurt, cheese, sour cream, and more. For those of you who like ice cream, avoid the sugar and the milk by going with a fresh fruit sorbet for dessert.

Avoid Red Meat

While protein is an important nutrient on the Mediterranean diet, it is important to pick the right kinds of protein to consume. Fish and other lean meats like chicken and turkey, are the best choices rather than eating a lot of meat. This is going to be a difference from your American diet, but it can help to keep you health. Eating a lot of red meat has been linked to a number of health conditions including:

- Chronic inflammation
- Heart disease
- Hypertension
- Diabetes
- Cancer
- Elevated cholesterol

If you decide to eat red meat, make sure that you do it once or twice a month, rather than every day. Go with leaner choices that don't have as much saturated fats or cholesterol inside of them. Protein and b-vitamins are important, but there are many more options you can go with rather than red meat.

Flavoring Your Meals

In the American diet, you are used to flavoring your meals with butter, bad oils, dressing, and salt. These can really add some flavoring to your meals, but they also add a lot of other nutrients that aren't good on the heart or the body. Choosing healthier options is a much better way to make your meals conform to the Mediterranean diet.

To start, cut out the salt as this can really mess with your blood pressure. Use garlic or onion powder or stick with black pepper to season the food. Olive oil is the best option when it comes to cooking your food. Instead of using sugar to sweeten up your desserts or side dishes, go with cinnamon as this can sweeten the food while helping to lower blood pressure and keeping your blood sugars in line.

Finding Desserts on the Mediterranean Diet

You don't have to completely miss out on the desserts that you enjoy on this diet, you just need to make some adjustments to keep it healthy on the body. You will need to avoid some desserts that are full of bad carbs, sugars, high fructose corn syrup, and other nutrients that are ruining our health. It is important to find snacks and desserts that are better while still hitting that sweet tooth.

The first thing you should reach for when you want something sweet is fruit. Fruits are so great with all the vitamins, nutrients, and antioxidants that your body needs to stay healthy. There are also natural sugars that make the fruit sweet, but which won't raise the blood sugar levels like cakes, cookies, and other desserts. You can add some onto your granola, eat it plain, or find another way to use this as a delicious snack.

Dark chocolate is an exception allowed on the Mediterranean diet. Remember this is for dark chocolate, not all chocolate. This kind of chocolate is the purest form that comes from cocoa beans which are full of flavonoids and antioxidants. Flavonoids are perfect for keeping your blood sugars level, balancing cholesterol, and lowering blood pressure. Plus, they can really make you feel good when giving into those sugar cravings. While you shouldn't have chocolate every day, indulging on occasion with a bit of dark chocolate can help you stick with the diet and still have your little treat.

The Mediterranean diet is there to help you give your body the nutrients that it really needs. Many times we get sick or deal with health issues because the foods we eat and the lifestyle we live are just not healthy. The Mediterranean diet will help us to take in healthy nutrients that will align our blood pressure, keep blood sugars balanced, reduce cholesterol, and get us in the best shape of our lives in terms of health. Following the recommendations listed in this chapter and the rest of the guidebook can ensure that you are keeping your body running functionally all the time.

Chapter 6: Putting the Mediterranean Diet to Use In Your Daily Life

Purchasing Foods on the Mediterranean Diet

Picking out the foods that you should purchase at the grocery store can be one of the hardest decisions. You want to make the right choices for your health, but once you get to the store, you may have more questions than answers when it comes to picking out the foods you will eat.

One of the best things that you can do to pick out good foods is to stick along the outer aisles at the grocery store. Don't go more than a few aisles deep on either side. The outer aisles are more likely to have the healthy and whole foods while the middle aisles are going to be full of the preservatives and unhealthy dessert and snack foods. Also, don't go shopping on an empty stomach because you are more likely to purchase things you shouldn't have when you're hungry.

Pastas, Breads, and Other Grains

Pastas, breads, and whole grains like oatmeal, quinoa, and barley, are great on this diet. You just need to make sure you pick whole grain options. These contain all of the grain kernel and will give you the fiber and other nutrients that the body needs. Avoid baked goods and other white breads that have been processed so much that all the nutrition is gone.

Protein Sources

When picking out your protein source, make sure that you stick with lean options. Cold water and oily fish are the best, such as tuna and salmon, although all fish can provide great nutrition and allows you to mix things up a bit at the dinner table. Chicken and turkey are good options as well to add in more dishes. A bit of red meat is allowed so if you want to have a special meal or need a change, bring home a bit with you.

Fruits and Vegetables

Fruits and vegetables are important to this diet program. Any fruit or vegetable or fruit that you can find in the produce section will help to keep you healthy and provide you with tons of antioxidants and nutrients. Try to mix up the types of produce you bring home to really get all the nutrients you need into your body.

Fresh is always the best, as long as it is in season and hasn't had to travel too far. Frozen is still pretty good and can be nice in the winter when there isn't much produce to pick from. Never go with canned fruits or vegetables because these are void of most of the nutrition that you expect from produce.

Nuts

Nuts are allowed on this diet plan and can be delicious as a snack or fit in well as a topping or breading on some of your meals. Almonds and walnuts are the best choices in terms of nutrition, but most will work. Remember that you need to eat nuts in moderation. They have a lot of the nutrition that you need, but too much can add too many calories and fat to your diet.

Oils

Stick with oils that are approved on this diet plan. Olive oil is the best while you should avoid butter and margarine. Olive oil provides much of the same flavoring that you find in the other options, but it is lower in calories, full of good vitamins, and so much healthier to use.

Preparing Your Meals

Homemade meals are key on this diet plan. It is unlikely that you will find your best choices in the freezer section or at a restaurant, although there are some choices that can work on occasion if you do need to eat out. Most of your meals should be made at home with fresh and whole ingredients. This may take some extra time, but meal planning can really make it better.

Planning ahead for the week can really help you keep on track. You could consider making enough lunches for a week and then leaving them in the freezer until you need them. Freezer meals also work well for those who have a busier night and won't get home to eat until later or just when you don't feel like cooking. Slow cookers, pressure cookers, or just modifying some of your old favorite recipes can really help too.

The best meals that you can make will be home cooked right when you need them as this will preserve the foods the best and make them nutritious. But for those times you are busy and need some help, planning ahead and using some other methods can really make things easier.

Sitting Down to Eat

Many American families are always on the run. They are not only busy at work during the day, but they have to come home to more activities that night, work during supper, and are always up to something else. There is rarely time to get a meal prepared much less sit down as a family and eat it without doing other things at the same time.

With the Mediterranean diet, you need to change some of these habits. It is not healthy to always eat on the run. It is not healthy to have so much going on in your life that you can't take a few minutes to sit back and relax. It is not healthy to always be on the run from one thing to another without taking time to truly enjoy your meal and the company you keep.

While on this diet plan, you will need to learn how to slow down. Meals are not just a way to provide sustenance in the Mediterranean area; rather they are big events that take time and allow you to sit back with family and friends. You will need to start implementing this in your life. No longer are you going to rush through your meal or eat alone. You will instead take some time to talk, laugh, and just enjoy the experience.

It may be hard to do this for every meal of the day, but consider making it a requirement for supper. Even if you need to have supper a bit later at night so everyone can be home, just sit down and enjoy the meal together. Have a few courses, talk about your day, share stories, and make sure that all the phones, computers, and other distractions are kept away. This may seem strange at first, but it will make a big difference in how relaxed you feel as well as how connected you feel to your family.

The Mediterranean diet is one that you need to implement as a lifestyle, not just as a few changes to the foods you eat. Preparing your meals properly, learning how to go to the grocery store and pick out the right foods, and spending time with friends and family while you eat, rather than just rushing out the door, will make it easier to see the benefits of this diet plan.

Chapter 7: Going Out to Eat on the Mediterranean Diet

For the most part, you should concentrate your efforts to eating at home. This is the easiest way to pick out meals that will stay healthy and follow the Mediterranean diet. Each time that you choose to go out of your home to have a meal, you are running into temptation that could derail all of your hard work and make you go back to your old habits.

Of course, there are going to be times when you decide that it is worth it to go out to eat. Perhaps it has been a long time and you are doing well on the diet. Your friends or family may have invited you out or there is a big event that you are celebration. It is not always possible to forego eating out all of the time, and having the right tools and information available can make it easier to stick with your diet plan even while indulging.

Tips to Eating Out

If you are going out to eat for a special occasion, keep some of these easy tips in mind to pick the right choices for your health while out of the home.

1. Never go to the restaurant feeling really hungry. Have some almonds or a small snack before going or drink some water. This helps to prevent you from ordering the biggest thing on the menu or eating all of the breadbasket while you are there.
2. Avoid the breadbasket. If you want a bit to eat before the meal, as for a small bit of whole grain bread and see if the kitchen will give you a bit of olive oil. This is much healthier than eating the whole breadbasket.
3. Avoid the red meat. This can be hard when sitting around others who are enjoying hamburgers or steaks, but it is not a good idea to go with these. Choose a dish with fish or some skinless poultry to stay healthy.
4. Anything that is fried is not allowed while on the diet. Broiled, baked, and grilled are the words you should look for when out to eat.
5. Frozen and processed foods are not really the best options unless you can't help it. Fresh food tastes so much better and will add more nutrients to your day.

6. Ask the kitchen whether any of the food is cooked in hydrogenated oils (trans fats). If your dish is cooked with this oil, make sure to avoid it.
7. If you are going with a dish that has pasta in it, ask if they would be willing to substitute in whole grain pasta.
8. For a healthy appetizer, or even the whole meal if you are watching calories, ask for a salad full of fresh vegetables with a bit of olive oil or balsamic dressing on top.
9. If at all possible, request that they give you some brown or whole grain rice rather than white rice.
10. Sodas and fruit drinks, or pretty much anything other than green tea or water, should be avoided at restaurants. These are normally full of sugars and calories, and they are always so much worse at a restaurant because they need to be preserved. Stick with the basics or bring along your own drink.
11. Never eat the whole portion. The portions at restaurants are always way bigger than you should eat. You should make sure to only eat half of it and then bring the rest home. Or even better, as you are placing your order, ask if they would wrap up half the order before they bring it to the table. This helps you to stop before going over your half limit.
12. If you decide to go for dessert, go with some fresh fruit. Be certain that it is fresh fruit though. There are many desserts that will add sugar or syrups and other ingredients to the fruit, basically making them just as bad as that cake, ice cream, or other dish you are trying to avoid.
13. If the restaurant offers it, consider having some hot green tea after the meal is done. This will allow you to cleanse the pallet and gives your body a bit of extra protection on the heart. You can also choose to do this when you get home if not available at your restaurant.
14. Plan ahead as much as possible. Many restaurants have their menus as well as nutritional information available online now. This means you can check out your options before even going in if you know where the meal is held. Pick out what you would like to eat with the confidence that it will fit on this diet plan.

Eating out can sometimes be a hassle while on a diet. You worry about whether you will find the right food options that taste good and fit with the diet or if you are going to indulge too much with your choices. But with a bit of careful planning and remembering some of these easy tips, you will find that it is easier than ever to eat out while on the Mediterranean diet.

Chapter 8: Making the Choice to Follow the Mediterranean Diet

When it comes to your health, you are the one in charge. You get to decide whether you are going to make the right choices and start exercising, reducing stress, and eating the right foods or if you will continue to live your current lifestyle until things get bad.

There are many people who feel they are invincible. They continue to eat the bad foods they enjoy, live a sedentary life, and do nothing to make a difference that would positively impact their health. These people assume they can make changes later. They are certain that they will be able to make the changes necessary once a problem shows up. They feel fine now, don't have any bad side effects from their choices at this moment, and that is all they need to worry about.

These people are going down a bad path. They will continue to eat the foods they like, going out to eat often and avoiding good nutrition, avoid taking medications to help because they think they don't need the pills or aren't able to avoid them, and avoiding exercise like it is some kind of plague. They are usually overweight, always tired, ready to snap at anyone because of all the stress, and headed straight to a heart attack.

The biggest issue here is that people in this mindset think they have time to make the changes necessary. In the back of their minds, they think that once the chest pain comes or the weakness in breath hits them, they will have the time to change their minds and their habits in order to get healthy. Unfortunately, while some may survive a heart attack and be able to make these changes later, others will end up dying at the first signs of a heart attack, making it too late to change their lifestyles.

It doesn't have to be this way. You can start your fight against heart disease right away. It doesn't matter how old or how young you are because everyone is at a risk for heart disease at some point in their lives and making the changes as soon as possible can really help. Think about it, cardiovascular disease claims the most lives compared to all other diseases and every 30 seconds, someone dies in America because of heart disease. Do you really want to leave it up to chance to see if you will live through your unhealthy lifestyle?

If you aren't worried about heart disease and the effect it can have on your body, go ahead and keep eating the foods that you do, all the trash that you find at that restaurant, the candies, baked goods and more. There is no set date when all of this will effect you, but eventually you will have a heart condition and the only warning signs you get could be your only ones.

The second option is to take a stand and get yourself to good health. Whether you have had health conditions in the past or you want to prevent them in the future, it is important to get started as soon as possible. The Mediterranean diet is the lifestyle change that you need for your health. Sure you won't be able to eat some of the foods that you used to enjoy and you will have to get up and get moving more often, but isn't the health of your heart worth it?

The Mediterranean diet has everything that you need to stay healthy and happy. It has whole foods that are chock full of the nutrients that your body needs to flush out toxins, work properly, and keep the heart strong. In addition to all the good foods you get to eat, you get the benefit of learning how to eliminate some of the foods that are hard on your body, the sugars, salts, trans fats, saturated fats, and more. You pick out the healthiest options so your body always works properly.

But as we've mentioned in this guidebook, it is not just about the foods you choose. The Mediterranean diet helps you to make all of the right decisions to keep your body working properly. For example, in addition to a healthy diet, the Mediterranean diet asks you to get going on a good exercise plan, spending at least thirty minutes three or four times a week up and moving as much as possible. This helps to strengthen the heart, burns more calories for weight loss, and improves your mood all in one.

Next comes stress reduction. While it may seem normal to have all this stress in your life in the modern world, it is doing the most damage to your health. Learning how to manage the stress, with good eating habits and exercise, meditation, yoga, or just relaxing, can do wonders for your heart and keeps you feeling young and vibrant.

When all of these different parts come together, you are going to see huge improvements in your health. You will reduce your risk of heart disease, cancer, obesity, diabetes, and more. Even if you already have some of these conditions, following the lifestyle changes in the

Mediterranean diet can still help you to control, and even eliminate, some of those health issues that are taking over your life. You can control your health; you just need to make the decision to do so.

So you have two choices. You can choose to keep living your unhealthy lifestyle, the one that has you eating out all of the time and never working out, the one that makes you sick and is just a ticking time bomb waiting for the heart attack to happen. Or you can choose to make a switch now to the Mediterranean diet and life a healthier and happier life with all the good lifestyle benefits that it provides. You choose.

102 Delicious Mediterranean Recipes

Breakfast
Egg Omelet from the Oven

Prep Time: 5 minutes; **Cook Time:** 25 minutes	
Serving Size: 248g; **Serves:** 4; **Calories:** 286	
Total Fat: 18.9g **Saturated Fat:** 8.9g; **Trans Fat:** 0g	
Protein: 20.3g; **Net Carbs:** 6.9g	
Total Carbs: 9g; **Dietary Fiber:** 2.1g; **Sugars:** 5g	
Cholesterol: 407mg; **Sodium:** 1064mg; **Potassium:** 345mg;	
Vitamin A: 31%; **Vitamin C:** 15%; **Calcium:** 24%; **Iron:** 16%.	

Ingredients:
- 8 eggs
- ½ cups milk
- ½ cups grated parmesan cheese
- ½ cups roasted red peppers, chopped
- ½ cups sun dried tomatoes, chopped
- 1 cup artichoke hearts, chopped
- 1 cup fresh baby spinach, chopped
- 1 teaspoon salt
- 1 tablespoon butter

Directions:
1. Preheat the oven to 350 degrees F.
2. In a large bowl, whisk together the eggs and milk. Toss in the grated parmesan, red peppers, dun dried tomatoes, artichoke hearts and fresh spinach. Season with salt.
3. Pour the mixture into a 9x9-inch dish and bake for 25 minutes.
4. Serve immediately.

Spinach Frittata

Prep Time: 10 minutes; **Cook Time:** 7 minutes	
Serving Size: 150g; **Serves:** 4; **Calories:** 183	
Total Fat: 12.1g **Saturated Fat:** 4.4g; **Trans Fat:** 0g	
Protein: 15.6g; **Net Carbs:** 2.4g	
Total Carbs: 2.9g; **Dietary Fiber:** 0.5g; **Sugars:** 1.8g	
Cholesterol: 294mg; **Sodium:** 348mg; **Potassium:** 237mg;	
Vitamin A: 22%; **Vitamin C:** 4%; **Calcium:** 9%; **Iron:** 10%.	

Ingredients:
- 2 teaspoons olive oil
- ¾ cup packed baby spinach
- 2 green onions
- 4 large egg whites
- 6 large eggs
- 1/3 cup crumbled feta cheese
- 1 tablespoon sun dried tomatoes, chopped
- salt, to taste

Directions:
1. Preheat the broiler.
2. Heat the olive oil in a skillet. In the meantime, chop the spinach and onions.
3. Combine the egg whites, eggs, feta cheese, dun dried tomatoes and salt in a medium bowl. Toss in the spinach and onions and stir well.
4. Pour the egg mixture into the pan and cook for about 2 minutes. Gently stir and cook for another 2 minutes.
5. Then, broil for 2 to 3 minutes.
6. Serve immediately.

Blueberry Quinoa

Prep Time: 5 minutes; **Cook Time:** 5 minutes

Serving Size: 262g; **Serves:** 4; **Calories:** 234

Total Fat: 9.1g **Saturated Fat:** 2.7g; **Trans Fat:** 0g

Protein: 9g; **Net Carbs:** 28.5g

Total Carbs: 31.6g; **Dietary Fiber:** 3.1g; **Sugars:** 14.2g

Cholesterol: 18mg; **Sodium:** 66mg; **Potassium:** 231mg;

Vitamin A: 0%; **Vitamin C:** 10%; **Calcium:** 4%; **Iron:** 9%.

Ingredients:
- 2 cups milk
- ½ teaspoon ground cinnamon
- 2 cups cooked quinoa
- 1 cup blueberries
- ¼ cup sliced almonds
- 1 tablespoon honey

Directions:
1. Whisk together the milk and cinnamon in a large bowl.
2. Scoop the cooked quinoa into 4 individual serving bowls.
3. Pour over the cinnamon milk and top with blueberries, almonds and honey.

Peanut Butter Banana Yogurt Bowl

Prep Time: 5 minutes; **Cook Time:** 5 minutes	
Serving Size: 308g; **Serves**: 4; **Calories:** 305	
Total Fat: 11.4g **Saturated Fat**: 1.8g; **Trans Fat:** 0g	
Protein: 28.5g; **Net Carbs:** 23.2g	
Total Carbs: 28.2g; **Dietary Fiber:** 5g; **Sugars:** 17.7g	
Cholesterol: 15mg; **Sodium**: 155mg; **Potassium**: 627mg;	
Vitamin A: 1%; **Vitamin C**: 8%; **Calcium**: 27%; **Iron**: 12%.	

Ingredients:
- ☐ 4 cups plain Greek yogurt
- ☐ 2 medium bananas, sliced
- ☐ ¼ cup creamy peanut butter
- ☐ ¼ cup flax seed meal
- ☐ cinnamon

Directions:

1. Divide the yogurt between 4 individual serving bowls and top it with sliced bananas.
2. Melt the peanut butter in a microwave and drizzle it over each bowl with yogurt and banana.
3. Sprinkle the top with flax seed meal and cinnamon to taste.

Egg Muffins with Vegetables and Parmesan Cheese

Prep Time: 20 minutes; **Cook Time:** 20 minutes
Serving Size: 192g; **Serves:** 2; **Calories:** 218
Total Fat: 12.9g **Saturated Fat:** 5.9g; **Trans Fat:** 0g
Protein: 18.2g; **Net Carbs:** 5.7g
Total Carbs: 7g; **Dietary Fiber:** 1.3g; **Sugars:** 1.6g
Cholesterol: 293mg; **Sodium:** 465mg; **Potassium:** 403mg;
Vitamin A: 29%; **Vitamin C:** 62%; **Calcium:** 31%; **Iron:** 21%.

Ingredients:
- olive oil, for greasing
- 3 large eggs
- 2 tablespoons milk
- 8 tablespoons grated Parmesan cheese
- 1 ounce leek, finely chopped
- 1 ounce baby spinach, finely chopped
- ¼ red pepper, finely chopped
- 1 tomato, chopped

Directions:
1. Preheat the oven to 375 degrees F and grease 6 muffin cups with olive oil.
2. In a medium bowl, whisk together the eggs, milk and 4 tablespoons of Parmesan cheese.
3. Toss all the chopped vegetables together and divide them among the 6 muffin cups.
4. Pour the eggs evenly into each cup filled with the vegetables. Top them with the remaining 4 tablespoons of Parmesan cheese.
5. Bake for about 15 to 20 minutes, until the eggs are set.

Couscous with Apricots and Pistachios

Prep Time: 5 minutes; **Cook Time:** 5 minutes
Serving Size: 327g; **Serves:** 3; **Calories:** 584
Total Fat: 11.4g **Saturated Fat:** 2.8g; **Trans Fat:** 0g
Protein: 19.7g; **Net Carbs:** 100.3g
Total Carbs: 107.8g; **Dietary Fiber:** 7.5g; **Sugars:** 43.4g
Cholesterol: 13mg; **Sodium:** 144mg; **Potassium:** 619mg;
Vitamin A: 25%; **Vitamin C**: 10%; **Calcium**: 23%; **Iron**: 16%.

Ingredients:
- ½ cup boiling water
- 2 cups milk
- 3 tablespoons honey
- 1 teaspoon cinnamon
- 1 ½ cup couscous, dry
- 2/3 cup dried apricots, roughly chopped
- 1/3 cup shelled pistachios, roughly chopped
- ½ cup fresh raspberries

Directions:
1. Pour the boiling water, cinnamon, 2 tablespoons of honey and 1 cup of milk in a deep pan and bring to a boil.
2. Remove from the stove and stir in the couscous. Cover with a lid and let it sit for about 5 minutes.
3. Remove the lid, stir the couscous and pour in the remaining milk, chopped apricots and pistachios. Cover with a lid again and let it sit for another 2 minutes.
4. Tip the couscous mixture into a large bowl and add the fresh raspberries and honey.

Baked Eggs from Tuscany

Prep Time: 5 minutes; **Cook Time:** 20 minutes
Serving Size: 338g; **Serves:** 2; **Calories:** 277
Total Fat: 18g **Saturated Fat:** 5.1g; **Trans Fat:** 0g
Protein: 16.5g; **Net Carbs:** 9.7g
Total Carbs: 13.4g; **Dietary Fiber:** 3.7g; **Sugars:** 9.1g
Cholesterol: 376mg; **Sodium:** 665mg; **Potassium:** 143mg;
Vitamin A: 29%; **Vitamin C:** 28%; **Calcium:** 16%; **Iron:** 14%.

Ingredients:
- 1 tablespoon olive oil
- ¼ cup chopped red onion
- 1 teaspoon minced garlic
- 1 (14.5-ounce) can diced tomatoes
- 4 eggs
- 2 tablespoons grated Parmesan cheese

Directions:
1. Heat the olive oil, toss in the chopped onion and sauté for 2 to 3 minutes.
2. Add the minced garlic and cook for about 1 more minute. Toss in the canned tomatoes simmer for about 6 to 8 minutes, until the tomato mixture thickens.
3. In the meantime, preheat your broiler.
4. When the tomatoes thicken, remove half of the mixture to a separate bowl. Spread the rest around the bottom of a pan and break the eggs into the same pan. Spoon the other half of the tomatoes over the egg whites, leaving the yolks showing.
5. Cover with a lid and let the eggs cook for about 5 to 7 minutes. When the eggs are almost done, sprinkle on the grated cheese and place under the broiler for 1 or 2 minutes.
6. Serve immediately.

Breakfast Vegetarian Sandwich

Prep Time: 15 minutes; **Cook Time:** 15 minutes
Serving Size: 205g; **Serves:** 4; **Calories:** 280
Total Fat: 11.6g **Saturated Fat:** 3.1g; **Trans Fat:** 0g
Protein: 11.7g; **Net Carbs:** 25.7g
Total Carbs: 30.4g; **Dietary Fiber:** 4.7g; **Sugars:** 3.8g
Cholesterol: 99mg; **Sodium:** 309mg; **Potassium:** 412mg;
Vitamin A: 7%; **Vitamin C:** 17%; **Calcium:** 17%; **Iron:** 9%.

Ingredients:

- 4 slices of focaccia bread
- 2 eggs
- 2 tablespoons plain Greek yogurt
- 4 leaves fresh spinach
- 4 tablespoons shredded mozzarella cheese
- 1 avocado
- 2 tablespoons lemon juice
- sun dried tomatoes, to taste
- 1 cucumber, sliced
- crumbled feta cheese, to taste

Directions:

1. Toast the bread. In the meantime, beat the yogurt and the egg in a small dish.
2. Pour the egg mixture in a pan and, while it cooks, fold it in the shape of the bread.
3. Add some spinach in the middle of the egg while it cooks and flip it over. Sprinkle with the mozzarella and cook until the cheese is melted.
4. Mash the avocado with lemon juice and spread it onto the toasted bread.
5. Layer the sandwich with the egg, sun dried tomatoes, sliced cucumber and feta cheese.

Sandwiches
Panera Mediterranean Veggie Sandwich

Prep Time: 15 minutes; **Cook Time:** 0 minutes	
Serving Size: 863g; **Serves:** 2; **Calories:** 506	
Total Fat: 9g **Saturated Fat:** 2.8g; **Trans Fat:** 0g	
Protein: 19.4g; **Net Carbs:** 81.6g	
Total Carbs: 90.3g; **Dietary Fiber:** 8.7g; **Sugars:** 14g	
Cholesterol: 15mg; **Sodium:** 1021mg; **Potassium:** 953mg;	
Vitamin A: 11%; **Vitamin C:** 81%; **Calcium:** 18%; **Iron:** 44%.	

Ingredients:
- 4 slices Panera tomato basil bread
- 4 tablespoons jalapeno hummus
- 4 leaves fresh lettuce
- 2 medium tomatoes, thinly sliced
- 2 cucumbers, thinly sliced
- 2 red onions, thinly sliced
- 2 tablespoons crumbled feta cheese
- 2 peppadew peppers, chopped

Directions:
1. Spread all bread slices with hummus.
2. Layer on the lettuce, tomato, cucumber and red onion slices. Sprinkle with feta cheese and peppadew peppers. Cover with the other bread slice.
3. Finish off by cutting the sandwiches in two.

Grilled Veggie Sandwich

Prep Time: 20 minutes; **Cook Time:** 5 minutes
Serving Size: 415g; **Serves:** 4; **Calories:** 357
Total Fat: 16.2g **Saturated Fat:** 3g; **Trans Fat:** 0g
Protein: 11g; **Net Carbs:** 36.8g
Total Carbs: 44.9g; **Dietary Fiber:** 8.1g; **Sugars:** 6.1g
Cholesterol: 9mg; **Sodium:** 346mg; **Potassium:** 762mg;
Vitamin A: 9%; **Vitamin C:** 89%; **Calcium:** 11%; **Iron:** 22%.

Ingredients:
- ¼ cup mayonnaise
- 2 garlic cloves, minced
- 2 small zucchini, thinly sliced lengthwise
- 2 portabella mushrooms, sliced
- 1 eggplant, sliced
- 2 tablespoons olive oil
- ¾ of a 1 pound ciabatta loaf, split horizontally
- 2 ounces feta cheese, crumbled
- 2 medium tomatoes, sliced
- 2 cups baby arugula

Directions:

1. Heat a grill to high and in the meantime, mix the mayonnaise and minced garlic into a sauce. Set aside.
2. Brush zucchini, mushrooms, and eggplant with olive oil and grill for about 3 minutes.
3. Grill the ciabatta cut side down for about 2 minutes.
4. Cut the ciabatta loaf into four pieces.
5. Spread the bottoms with the mayonnaise sauce and spread the tops with feta cheese.
6. Layer the bottom with sliced zucchini, mushrooms, eggplant, tomatoes and arugula and cover with the tops.

Sandwich Loaded with Green Veggies

Prep Time: 15 minutes; **Cook Time:** 0 minutes	
Serving Size: 223g; **Serves:** 2; **Calories:** 239	
Total Fat: 6.2g **Saturated Fat:** 0.9g; **Trans Fat:** 0g	
Protein: 12.7g; **Net Carbs:** 34.1g	
Total Carbs: 41.7g; **Dietary Fiber:** 7.6g; **Sugars:** 10.8g	
Cholesterol: 5mg; **Sodium:** 445mg; **Potassium:** 239mg;	
Vitamin A: 12%; **Vitamin C:** 48%; **Calcium:** 15%; **Iron:** 12%.	

Ingredients:
- ☐ 4 slices whole wheat bread
- ☐ 4 tablespoons cilantro jalapeno hummus
- ☐ 2 whole leaves fresh lettuce
- ☐ ½ cup sprouts
- ☐ 4 large tomato slices
- ☐ 4 cucumber slices
- ☐ 1 red onion, thinly sliced
- ☐ 2 tablespoons crumbled feta cheese
- ☐ 4 Peppadew peppers, chopped

Directions:
1. Spread both slices of bread with hummus.
2. Layer the bottom half with lettuce, sprouts, tomato, cucumber and red onion slices, feta cheese and peppers. Cover with the tops.
3. If you wish, you can cut each sandwich in half before serving.

Mediterranean Picnic Sandwich

Prep Time: 15 minutes; **Cook Time:** 8 minutes

Serving Size: 307g; **Serves:** 4; **Calories:** 347

Total Fat: 22.6g **Saturated Fat:** 3.3g; **Trans Fat:** 0g

Protein: 8.3g; **Net Carbs:** 24.5g

Total Carbs: 31.8g; **Dietary Fiber:** 7.3g; **Sugars:** 11.1g

Cholesterol: 5mg; **Sodium:** 217mg; **Potassium:** 519mg;

Vitamin A: 6%; **Vitamin C:** 27%; **Calcium:** 9%; **Iron:** 5%.

Ingredients:
- 1 small eggplant, sliced
- 1 small zucchini, sliced
- 1 small yellow squash, sliced
- 3 tablespoons olive oil
- 1 loaf ciabatta bread, halved
- ⅓ cup prepared pesto
- ⅓ cup prepared tapenade
- 8 ounces fresh mozzarella, drained and thinly sliced
- 2 tablespoons balsamic vinegar

Directions:

1. Heat a grill or grill pan and brush the sliced eggplant, zucchini and yellow squash with 2/3 of the olive oil. Grill for 3 to 4 minutes per side and transfer to plate.
2. Hollow the ciabatta and spread pesto to one side of it. Spread the tapenade on the other side.
3. Place the grilled eggplant, zucchini, yellow squash and mozzarella on one side of the ciabatta. Drizzle everything with balsamic vinegar and the remaining olive oil.
4. Cover with the other half of the ciabatta and wrap the sandwich in a plastic wrap.
5. Transfer to a baking sheet and cover with a heavy skillet or cans. Refrigerate it pressed down for at least 2 hours or even overnight.
6. Slice into 4 sandwiches before serving.

Classic Pita Sandwich

Prep Time: 15 minutes; **Cook Time:** 0 minutes	
Serving Size: 142g; **Serves:** 2; **Calories:** 226	
Total Fat: 8.4g; **Saturated Fat:** 2.8g; **Trans Fat:** 0g	
Protein: 10.6g; **Net Carbs:** 22.6g	
Total Carbs: 28.6g; **Dietary Fiber:** 6g; **Sugars:** 1.3g	
Cholesterol: 15mg; **Sodium:** 582mg; **Potassium:** 331mg;	
Vitamin A: 69%; **Vitamin C:** 3%; **Calcium:** 12%; **Iron:** 13%.	

Ingredients:
- [ ] 1 whole wheat pita, sliced in half
- [ ] ¼ cup hummus
- [ ] ¼ cup shredded carrots
- [ ] ½ cup fresh baby spinach
- [ ] ¼ cup canned chickpeas, drained
- [ ] 2 tablespoons crumbled feta cheese
- [ ] 1 tablespoon chopped black olives
- [ ] salt and pepper, to taste

Directions:
1. Spread the hummus inside each pita pocket.
2. Divide the carrots, spinach, chickpeas, feta cheese and olives equally between the two pockets.
3. Best served fresh.

Grilled Turkey Sandwich

Prep Time: 15 minutes; **Cook Time:** 10 minutes
Serving Size: 164g; **Serves**: 6; **Calories:** 349
Total Fat: 18.9g **Saturated Fat**: 5.2g; **Trans Fat**: 0g
Protein: 14.9g; **Net Carbs:** 25.2g
Total Carbs: 26.5g; **Dietary Fiber:** 1.3g; **Sugars:** 2.9g
Cholesterol: 41mg; **Sodium:** 839mg; **Potassium**: 131mg;
Vitamin A: 3%; **Vitamin C**: 16%; **Calcium**: 7%; **Iron**: 16%.

Ingredients:
- ¼ cup mayonnaise
- ¼ cup basil pesto
- 1 (1-pound) loaf ciabatta bread, sliced in half
- ½ pound deli turkey, thinly sliced
- ¾ cup roasted red pepper strips
- ¾ cup chopped black olives
- 6 slices provolone cheese

Directions:
1. Heat a grill or grill pan. In the meantime, combine the mayonnaise and pesto to make a sauce.
2. Spread the sauce over both sides of the ciabatta.
3. Layer the bottom half with turkey slices, red pepper strips, black olives and provolone cheese. Cover with the top half.
4. Wrap the sandwich in aluminum foil and place it onto the grill. Grill for about 10 to 15 minutes, until the cheese melts.
5. Slice the ciabatta into 6 sandwiches before serving.

Tuna Sandwich with Hummus

Prep Time: 15 minutes; **Cook Time:** 10 minutes
Serving Size: 120g; **Serves:** 4; **Calories:** 232
Total Fat: 10.6g **Saturated Fat:** 1.7g; **Trans Fat:** 0g
Protein: 17.3g; **Net Carbs:** 13.6g
Total Carbs: 16.6g; **Dietary Fiber:** 3g; **Sugars:** 1.7g
Cholesterol: 15mg; **Sodium:** 442mg; **Potassium:** 232mg;
Vitamin A: 1%; **Vitamin C:** 3%; **Calcium:** 4%; **Iron:** 8%.

Ingredients:
- 1 (7-ounce) can of tuna in oil
- ½ tablespoon diced green onion
- 1 tablespoon minced gherkin pickles
- 1 tablespoon lemon juice
- 1 tablespoon mayonnaise
- 1 tablespoon reserved oil from tuna
- ½ teaspoon Dijon mustard
- ¼ cup cannellini beans, drained
- 4 slices whole wheat bread
- hummus, to taste

Directions:
1. Drain the oil from the tuna and keep the oil.
2. Transfer the tuna in a bowl and mash it with a fork. Add the diced onion, pickles, lemon juice, mayonnaise, tuna oil and mustard and mix very well. In the end, add in the beans and slowly stir.
3. Spread the slices of bread with as much hummus as you wish. On top of that, spread the tuna mixture. Serve right away.

Chicken Sandwich

Prep Time: 4 hours; **Cook Time:** 30 minutes	
Serving Size: 363g; **Serves:** 4; **Calories:** 504	
Total Fat: 12.1g **Saturated Fat:** 3g; **Trans Fat:** 0g	
Protein: 37.2g; **Net Carbs:** 53.1g	
Total Carbs: 56.3g; **Dietary Fiber:** 3.2g; **Sugars:** 5.5g	
Cholesterol: 79mg; **Sodium:** 1454mg; **Potassium:** 502mg;	
Vitamin A: 4%; **Vitamin C:** 12%; **Calcium:** 24%; **Iron:** 3%.	

Ingredients:
- 4 skinless, boneless chicken breasts halves
- 1 cup buttermilk
- 2 teaspoons salt
- 1 teaspoon curry
- 1 large cucumber thinly sliced
- ½ small red onion, thinly sliced
- 1 tablespoon light sour cream
- 1 teaspoon fresh lemon juice
- 1 tablespoon plain Greek yogurt
- 2 tablespoons hummus
- 8 slices artisan bread
- 1 tablespoon olive oil

Directions:

1. Place the chicken, buttermilk, salt and curry in a plastic bag and turn to coat the meat. Let it chill for at least 4 hours.
2. Heat the grill. In the meantime, toss the sliced cucumber, onion, sour cream, lemon juice and yogurt in a bowl and stir.
3. Grill the chicken breasts for about 5 to 7 minutes per side.
4. Brush the bread slices with olive oil and grill for about 2 minutes per side. Spread with hummus and layer four slices of bread with chicken breast and homemade tzatziki. Cover with the remaining four slices of bread.

Super Simple Tuna Sandwich

Prep Time: 15 minutes; **Cook Time:** 0 minutes

Serving Size: 200g; **Serves:** 4; **Calories:** 316

Total Fat: 14.9g **Saturated Fat:** 2.3g; **Trans Fat:** 0g

Protein: 18.3g; **Net Carbs:** 22.7g

Total Carbs: 26.9g; **Dietary Fiber:** 4.7g; **Sugars:** 4.9g

Cholesterol: 12mg; **Sodium:** 290mg; **Potassium:** 359mg;

Vitamin A: 1%; **Vitamin C:** 16%; **Calcium:** 7%; **Iron:** 16%.

Ingredients:
- ¼ cup olive oil
- ½ cup red wine vinegar
- 1 red onion, very thinly sliced
- 1 (7-ounce) can of tuna in oil
- capers, to taste
- sliced Kalamata olives, to taste
- 1 fresh tomato, sliced 1/4-inch thick
- leafy greens, to taste
- 8 slices whole wheat bread

Directions:
1. In a smaller bowl, mix the olive oil with red wine vinegar. Toss in the sliced onion to marinate.
2. When done, drizzle four bread slices with the oil-vinegar mixture and layer with onion slices.
3. Continue with tuna, capers, olives, sliced tomato and leafy greens. Cover with the remaining four bread slices.
4. Press everything firmly together and let it rest for a few minutes before serving.

Avocado Tuna Sandwich

Prep Time: 20 minutes; **Cook Time:** 0 minutes	
Serving Size: 307g; **Serves**: 4; **Calories:** 430	
Total Fat: 16.9g **Saturated Fat**: 2.6g; **Trans Fat**: 0g	
Protein: 32g; **Net Carbs:** 28.4g	
Total Carbs: 40g; **Dietary Fiber:** 11.6g; **Sugars:** 6g	
Cholesterol: 25mg; **Sodium**: 346mg; **Potassium**: 898mg;	
Vitamin A: 4%; **Vitamin C**: 32%; **Calcium**: 10%; **Iron**: 23%.	

Ingredients:
- 2 ripe avocados, peeled and mashed
- 2 tablespoons lemon juice
- ¼ cup roasted red pepper strips, fresh or jarred
- 2 tablespoons chopped fresh parsley
- 2 (5-ounce) cans of tuna in water
- 8 slices multi-grain bread
- 8 tomato slices
- 8 slices red onions

Directions:
1. Combine the mashed avocado, lemon juice, red pepper strips and parsley in a medium bowl.
2. Flake the tuna and gently fold it in.
3. Layer four bread slices with 2 tomato slices, 2 onion slices and ¼ of the avocado spread. Cover with the remaining four bread slices.
4. Best served fresh.

Tuna Sandwich with Walnuts

Prep Time: 20 minutes; **Cook Time:** 0 minutes	
Serving Size: 307g; **Serves:** 2; **Calories:** 626	
Total Fat: 31.9g **Saturated Fat:** 3.7g; **Trans Fat:** 0g	
Protein: 56.3g; **Net Carbs:** 23.8g	
Total Carbs: 30.6g; **Dietary Fiber:** 6.8g; **Sugars:** 4.3g	
Cholesterol: 50mg; **Sodium:** 777mg; **Potassium:** 661mg;	
Vitamin A: 3%; **Vitamin C:** 3%; **Calcium:** 10%; **Iron:** 27%.	

Ingredients:
- 2 (4-ounce) cans tuna, drained
- 6 tablespoons roughly chopped cornichons
- 6 tablespoons roughly chopped walnuts
- 2 tablespoons olive oil
- 4 tablespoons mustard
- 4 slices multi-grain bread, toasted
- 2 fresh lettuce leaves, for serving

Directions:
1. Mix flaked tuna, chopped cornichons, walnuts, olive oil and mustard in a medium bowl.
2. Spread on all 4 slices of bread and layer lettuce on bottom halves of the sandwich. Cover with top halves and serve fresh.

Quick Chicken Pita Sandwich

Prep Time: 15 minutes; **Cook Time:** 5 minutes
Serving Size: 444g; **Serves:** 4; **Calories:** 518
Total Fat: 19.3g **Saturated Fat:** 4.6g; **Trans Fat:** 0g
Protein: 49.9g; **Net Carbs:** 33.1g
Total Carbs: 38.1g; **Dietary Fiber:** 5g; **Sugars:** 4.9g
Cholesterol: 105mg; **Sodium:** 388mg; **Potassium:** 370mg;
Vitamin A: 4%; **Vitamin C:** 33%; **Calcium:** 11%; **Iron:** 26%.

Ingredients:

- ½ teaspoon ground cumin
- ½ teaspoon garlic powder
- ½ teaspoon paprika
- 1 tablespoon olive oil
- 1 ½ pounds boneless, skinless chicken breasts, diced
- 5 ounces plain Greek yogurt
- 2 tablespoons olive oil
- 4 pieces of pita bread
- 1 large cucumber, peeled and thinly sliced
- 2 large tomatoes, sliced
- ¼ cup crumbled feta cheese

Directions:

1. Mix together the cumin, garlic powder, paprika and 1 tablespoon of olive oil in a large bowl. Toss in the diced chicken pieces and stir well to coat.
2. Heat a skillet and add the chicken in a single layer. Let it cook for 2 minutes, stir and cook for another 2 to 3 minutes.
3. While the chicken is cooking, whisk together the yogurt and olive oil. Season with salt and pepper to taste.
4. When the chicken is done, assemble the sandwiches. Spread the yogurt sauce over each pita bread, layer with chicken, sliced cucumber and tomatoes, and sprinkle with feta cheese.

Chicken Sandwich with Goat Cheese

Prep Time: 15 minutes; **Cook Time:** 5 minutes	
Serving Size: 269g; **Serves:** 6; **Calories:** 423	
Total Fat: 19.3g **Saturated Fat:** 5.6g; **Trans Fat:** 0g	
Protein: 32.6g; **Net Carbs:** 25.8g	
Total Carbs: 27.5g; **Dietary Fiber:** 1.7g; **Sugars:** 2.2g	
Cholesterol: 74mg; **Sodium:** 435mg; **Potassium:** 108mg;	
Vitamin A: 6%; **Vitamin C:** 15%; **Calcium:** 4%; **Iron:** 12%.	

Ingredients:
- 1 ¼ pounds boneless, skinless chicken breasts
- ½ cup balsamic vinaigrette, divided
- 1 loaf ciabatta bread
- olive oil, to taste
- 4 ounces soft goat cheese
- ¼ cup roasted red peppers
- 12 Kalamata olives
- 1-2 medium tomatoes, thinly sliced
- ½ cup sliced red onions
- 1 (0.75 ounce) package fresh arugula

Directions:
1. Place the chicken and ½ cup vinaigrette in a plastic bag and turn to coat the meat. Let it chill for at least 30 minutes or even overnight.
2. Heat the grill to medium and remove the chicken from the marinade. Grill the chicken for 5 to 6 minutes per side.
3. When done, let it cool for about 5 minutes, then slice it to ½-inch slices.
4. Slice the ciabatta in half horizontally and brush it with olive oil.
5. Grill the bread for about 2 to 3 minutes.
6. In the meantime, combine the goat cheese, peppers, olives and the remaining vinaigrette in a food processor. Process until thoroughly combined.
7. Spread this mixture on both pieces of ciabatta. Layer with sliced tomato, onion, arugula and chicken. Cover with the other half of the ciabatta.
8. Cut the sandwich into 6 parts before serving.

Chicken Pita Sandwich

Prep Time: 10 minutes; **Cook Time:** 0 minutes

Serving Size: 90g; **Serves:** 4; **Calories:** 193

Total Fat: 7.5g **Saturated Fat:** 2.6g; **Trans Fat:** 0g

Protein: 12.8g; **Net Carbs:** 16.5g

Total Carbs: 19.4g; **Dietary Fiber:** 2.9g; **Sugars:** 0.4g

Cholesterol: 39mg; **Sodium:** 469mg; **Potassium:** 82mg;

Vitamin A: 3%; **Vitamin C:** 3%; **Calcium:** 5%; **Iron:** 9%.

Ingredients:

- 4-5 ounces cooked rotisserie chicken
- ⅛ cup diced cucumber
- 2 tablespoons crumbled feta
- 2 tablespoons roasted red pepper, diced
- 1 tablespoon lemon juice
- salt and pepper, to taste
- ⅛ cup hummus
- 2 whole wheat pitas, sliced in half

Directions:

1. Toss together the chicken, diced cucumber, crumbled feta, red pepper and lemon juice in a medium bowl, and season with salt and pepper.
2. Spread the hummus inside both pitas and fill them with the chicken mixture. Slice in half and serve right away.

Chicken

Stuffed Chicken

Prep Time: 10 minutes; **Cook Time:** 25 minutes	
Serving Size: 166g; **Serves:** 4; **Calories:** 270	
Total Fat: 16.8g **Saturated Fat:** 4.6g; **Trans Fat:** 0g	
Protein: 28.2g; **Net Carbs:** 1g	
Total Carbs: 1.6g; **Dietary Fiber:** 0.6g; **Sugars:** 0.5g	
Cholesterol: 85mg; **Sodium:** 335mg; **Potassium:** 306mg;	
Vitamin A: 3%; **Vitamin C:** 80%; **Calcium:** 17%; **Iron:** 4%.	

Ingredients:
- ½ cup crumbled feta cheese
- 1 roasted red pepper
- 1 tablespoon chopped fresh basil
- 1 tablespoon chopped fresh parsley
- 4 boneless, skinless chicken breasts
- 1 garlic clove, minced
- salt and pepper, to taste
- 2 tablespoons olive oil
- ½ cup chicken broth

Directions:
1. Preheat the oven to 450 degrees F. Roast the red pepper in your oven for about 30 minutes. Let it rest for about 10 minutes, so the skin peels off easily. Chop the pepper and set it aside.
2. Put each chicken breast in a zip bag and pound it with a meat mallet to 1/4 -inch thick. Season well with salt, pepper and minced garlic.
3. In a separate bowl, toss together the feta cheese, diced red pepper, fresh basil and parsley.
4. Fill the breasts evenly with the filling and use a toothpick to keep the chicken shut while baking.
5. Heat the olive oil in a non-stick skillet, add the chicken and cook for 2 to 3 minutes per side.
6. Reduce the heat and pour in the chicken broth. Let it simmer for another 8 to 10 minutes.
7. Before serving, remove the toothpicks.

Chicken Breasts with Mozzarella

Prep Time: 10 minutes; **Cook Time:** 18 minutes
Serving Size: 256g; **Serves:** 4; **Calories:** 282
Total Fat: 14.6g **Saturated Fat:** 4.4g; **Trans Fat:** 0g
Protein: 28.6g; **Net Carbs:** 5.7g
Total Carbs: 7.1g; **Dietary Fiber:** 1.4g; **Sugars:** 3.8g
Cholesterol: 86mg; **Sodium:** 564mg; **Potassium:** 611mg;
Vitamin A: 9%; **Vitamin C:** 25%; **Calcium:** 16%; **Iron:** 5%.

Ingredients:

- 4 small boneless skinless chicken breasts
- 1 red onion, sliced
- 1 zucchini, chopped
- ¼ cup Italian dressing
- ½ cup grape tomatoes, halved
- ½ cup black olives, halved
- 1 cup shredded mozzarella cheese

Directions:

1. Heat a large skillet on medium heat and add the chicken breasts. Cover with a lid and let it cook for 5 to 7 minutes. Add the sliced onion and zucchini, turn the chicken and cook for another 5 to 7 minutes on the other side.
2. Pour in the dressing, grape tomatoes and olives. Cover with a lid and cook for another 2 minutes. Stir well.
3. Sprinkle with mozzarella, cover again and cook for another 2 minutes, or until the cheese is melted.

Simple Oven Chicken

Prep Time: 10 minutes; **Cook Time:** 25 minutes	
Serving Size: 287g; **Serves:** 4; **Calories:** 309	
Total Fat: 10.6g **Saturated Fat:** 1g; **Trans Fat:** 0g	
Protein: 19g; **Net Carbs:** 30.5g	
Total Carbs: 33.9g; **Dietary Fiber:** 3.4g; **Sugars:** 2.4g	
Cholesterol: 48mg; **Sodium:** 135mg; **Potassium:** 837mg;	
Vitamin A: 1%; **Vitamin C:** 104%; **Calcium:** 3%; **Iron:** 7%.	

Ingredients:
- ☐ 3 chicken breasts
- ☐ 2 tablespoons olive oil
- ☐ 2 tablespoons Italian seasoning
- ☐ salt and pepper, to taste
- ☐ 2 big potatoes, diced
- ☐ 1 red pepper, diced
- ☐ 1 small onion, diced
- ☐ 5 cloves garlic
- ☐ ½ cup black olives, halved

Directions:
1. Preheat the oven to 450 degrees F.
2. Line a baking sheet with parchment paper.
3. Add the chicken breast, 1 tablespoon of the olive oil, seasoning, salt and pepper in a medium bowl and coat the chicken.
4. In a separate bowl, mix all the vegetables, whole garlic cloves and the remaining 1 tablespoon of olive oil. Stir well.
5. Place the vegetables and chicken breasts with olives on the baking sheet and bake for 20 to 25 minutes, until the chicken is tender.

Grilled Chicken Breasts

Prep Time: 20 minutes; **Cook Time:** 15 minutes
Serving Size: 125g; **Serves:** 4; **Calories:** 263
Total Fat: 17.1g **Saturated Fat:** 3.3g; **Trans Fat:** 0g
Protein: 25.2g; **Net Carbs:** 1.4g
Total Carbs: 1.5g; **Dietary Fiber:** 0.1g; **Sugars:** 0.3g
Cholesterol: 75mg; **Sodium:** 273mg; **Potassium:** 274mg;
Vitamin A: 0%; **Vitamin C:** 6%; **Calcium:** 15%; **Iron:** 2%.

Ingredients:
- 4 (1-pound) boneless, skinless chicken breasts
- 3 tablespoons lemon juice
- 3 tablespoons olive oil
- 3 garlic cloves, minced
- ½ teaspoon dried oregano
- ½ teaspoon salt
- ½ teaspoon pepper

Directions:

1. Mix together the lemon juice, olive oil, garlic and oregano in large plastic bag.
2. Pierce the chicken breasts with a fork and season them with salt and pepper. Add them in the plastic bag and coat them with the dressing. Let it marinate for at least 20 minutes.
3. When done, grill the chicken for about 5 to 6 minutes per side.

Greek Lemon Chicken

Prep Time: 10 minutes; **Cook Time:** 30 minutes

Serving Size: 131g; **Serves:** 4; **Calories:** 151

Total Fat: 5.9g **Saturated Fat:** 0.3g; **Trans Fat:** 0g

Protein: 21.4g; **Net Carbs:** 1.5g

Total Carbs: 1.8g; **Dietary Fiber:** 0.3g; **Sugars:** 0.4g

Cholesterol: 64mg; **Sodium:** 126mg; **Potassium:** 398mg;

Vitamin A: 1%; **Vitamin C:** 18%; **Calcium:** 1%; **Iron:** 2%.

Ingredients:
- 4 small chicken breasts
- juice of 1 lemon
- 1 clove garlic, minced
- 1 tablespoon fresh oregano, finely chopped
- 1/2 tablespoon olive oil
- salt and pepper, to taste
- 10 black olives, halved
- ½ lemon, thinly sliced into 4 rounds and cut in half

Directions:

1. In a small bowl, mix together the lemon juice, minced garlic, oregano, olive oil, salt and pepper. Add the chicken breasts and let it marinate for 30 minutes or even overnight.
2. Preheat the oven to 375 degrees F. Arrange the breasts in a baking dish, discard the extra marinade, sprinkle with olives and arrange 2 lemon slices per chicken breast.
3. Bake for 30 to 40 minutes, until the meat is nicely tender.

Chicken Tomato Soup

Prep Time: 5 minutes; **Cook Time:** 35 minutes
Serving Size: 1506g; **Serves:** 4; **Calories:** 333
Total Fat: 13.7g **Saturated Fat:** 2.6g; **Trans Fat:** 0g
Protein: 25g; **Net Carbs:** 22.7g
Total Carbs: 30.4g; **Dietary Fiber:** 7.7g; **Sugars:** 9.4g
Cholesterol: 0mg; **Sodium:** 3728mg; **Potassium:** 1923mg;
Vitamin A: 16%; **Vitamin C:** 247%; **Calcium:** 7%; **Iron:** 68%.

Ingredients:

- 16 cups chicken stock
- 8 large tomatoes, diced
- 3 bell peppers, diced
- 3 zucchini, diced
- 5 ounces concentrated tomato puree
- 3 ounces capers
- 2 large onions, diced
- 4 cloves garlic, minced
- 2 tablespoons olive oil
- salt and pepper, to taste

Directions:

1. Heat the chicken stock, add the tomatoes, peppers and tomato puree. Bring to a boil, reduce the heat and let it simmer for 10 minutes.
2. Add the zucchini and capers and let it simmer for another 10 minutes.
3. In the meantime, heat the olive oil in a pan, add the onion and garlic and sauté for about 5 minutes.
4. Stir the fried onion and garlic into the soup and let it simmer for another 10 minutes.

Chicken with Polenta

Prep Time: 5 minutes; **Cook Time:** 12 minutes	
Serving Size: 596g; **Serves:** 4; **Calories:** 415	
Total Fat: 7.7g **Saturated Fat:** 2.6g; **Trans Fat:** 0g	
Protein: 36.6g; **Net Carbs:** 41g	
Total Carbs: 48.7g; **Dietary Fiber:** 7.4g; **Sugars:** 20.7g	
Cholesterol: 73mg; **Sodium:** 797mg; **Potassium:** 952mg;	
Vitamin A: 397%; **Vitamin C:** 106%; **Calcium:** 28%; **Iron:** 27%.	

Ingredients:
- olive oil, for greasing
- 1 pound chicken breast fillets
- 1 (14-ounce) jar tomato pasta sauce
- 12 black olives, chopped
- ¼ cup chopped parsley
- 2 2/3 cups milk
- 2/3 cup polenta
- 1 pound carrots, cut in matchsticks
- 10 ounces sugar snap peas, steamed

Directions:
1. Grease a pan with oil and sear the chicken for 1 to 2 minutes per side. Remove from the heat. Pour the tomato pasta sauce to pan and bring it to a boil. Let it simmer on low heat, covered with a lid, for about 5 minutes. Toss in the chopped olives and parsley
2. In the meantime, boil the milk, add polenta and cook over low heat for 3 to 4 minutes.
3. Serve the chicken with the sauce and vegetables.

Quick Chicken with Vegetables

Prep Time: 15 minutes; **Cook Time:** 35 minutes	
Serving Size: 597g; **Serves:** 2; **Calories:** 288	
Total Fat: 7g **Saturated Fat**: 1.8g; **Trans Fat**: 0g	
Protein: 29.3g; **Net Carbs:** 23g	
Total Carbs: 30.8g; **Dietary Fiber:** 7.8g; **Sugars:** 9.3g	
Cholesterol: 75mg; **Sodium:** 123mg; **Potassium:** 1198mg;	
Vitamin A: 5%; **Vitamin C**: 941%; **Calcium:** 15%; **Iron**: 86%.	

Ingredients:
- 2 boneless, skinless chicken breasts
- 1 tablespoon dried oregano
- 1 teaspoon black pepper
- 6 mini bell peppers, chopped
- 2 medium tomatoes, diced
- 2 jalapeño peppers, sliced
- 2 green onions, sliced

Directions:
1. Preheat the oven to 450 degrees F.
2. Season the chicken breasts with oregano and pepper, then place them in a baking dish.
3. Arrange all the vegetables around them, cover with tin foil and bake for about 35 minutes.
4. Uncover the foil, set the oven to broil and cook under the broiler for another 5 minutes.
5. Serve sliced chicken breasts with baked vegetables.

Chicken from a Skillet

Prep Time: 10 minutes; **Cook Time:** 25 minutes
Serving Size: 385g; **Serves:** 4; **Calories:** 342
Total Fat: 13.3g **Saturated Fat:** 3.3g; **Trans Fat:** 0g
Protein: 40.2g; **Net Carbs:** 12.6g
Total Carbs: 15.8g; **Dietary Fiber:** 3.2g; **Sugars:** 5.8g
Cholesterol: 99mg; **Sodium:** 389mg; **Potassium:** 120mg;
Vitamin A: 12%; **Vitamin C:** 71%; **Calcium:** 3%; **Iron:** 11%.

Ingredients:
- ¼ cup flour
- 1 teaspoon basil leaves
- ½ teaspoon oregano leaves
- ½ teaspoon rosemary leaves
- 1 ½ pounds boneless, skinless chicken breasts
- 2 tablespoon olive oil
- 1 large onion, cut into wedges
- 1 large green pepper, cut into strips
- 1 (14 ½-ounce) can diced tomatoes, undrained
- ½ cup chicken broth

Directions:

1. Mix the flour, basil, oregano and rosemary in a bowl and reserve 2 tablespoons f the mixture Use the rest to coat the chicken.
2. Heat the olive oil in a skillet and cook the chicken for 3 minutes each side.
3. Transfer the chicken to a plate and set aside. Use the same skillet to sauté the onion and pepper. Add the tomatoes, chicken broth and the reserved spices. Bring everything to a boil.
4. Place the chicken back into the skillet and let it simmer for about 10 minutes on low heat.

Garlic Lemon Herb Chicken

Prep Time: 90 minutes; **Cook Time:** 45 minutes
Serving Size: 516g; **Serves:** 4; **Calories:** 470
Total Fat: 20g **Saturated Fat:** 4.5g; **Trans Fat:** 0g
Protein: 28g; **Net Carbs:** 49.5g
Total Carbs: 57g; **Dietary Fiber:** 7.5g; **Sugars:** 8g
Cholesterol: 90mg; **Sodium:** 1243mg; **Potassium:** 471mg;
Vitamin A: 4%; **Vitamin C:** 192%; **Calcium:** 7%; **Iron:** 21%.

Ingredients:

- 4 skin-on, bone-in chicken thighs
- juice of 1 lemon
- 3 tablespoons olive oil
- 1 tablespoon red wine vinegar
- 4 large garlic cloves, minced
- 3 teaspoons dried basil
- 2 teaspoons dried oregano
- 2 teaspoons dried parsley
- 2 teaspoons salt, or to taste
- 8 baby potatoes, halved
- 1 red onion, sliced
- 1 red bell pepper, sliced
- 1 large zucchini, sliced

Directions:

1. Soak excess liquid from the chicken thighs. Mix lemon juice, 2 tablespoons of olive oil, vinegar, garlic, basil, oregano, parsley and salt. Pour half of the marinade to a dish and store the other half.
2. Add the thighs into the dish and coat in the sauce. Let it soak for 15 to 60 minutes; you can even do it overnight.
3. Preheat the oven to 430 degrees F. Heat 1 tablespoon of olive oil in a skillet over medium heat and sear the chicken for about 4 minutes on each side.
4. Spread the veggies around each thigh and pour the rest of the marinade over the meat.
5. Cover the dish with a lid and bake for about 35 minutes. Then, broil on medium heat for another 5 to 10 minutes, to make the chicken crispier.
6. Decorate with some lemon slices before serving.

Chicken with Basil Risotto

Prep Time: 15 minutes; **Cook Time:** 40 minutes	
Serving Size: 411g; **Serves:** 4; **Calories:** 532	
Total Fat: 23g **Saturated Fat:** 5.8g; **Trans Fat:** 0g	
Protein: 29g; **Net Carbs:** 48.2g	
Total Carbs: 51.4g; **Dietary Fiber:** 3.2g; **Sugars:** 2.6g	
Cholesterol: 94mg; **Sodium:** 932mg; **Potassium:** 675mg;	
Vitamin A: 7%; **Vitamin C:** 24%; **Calcium:** 12%; **Iron:** 13%.	

Ingredients:
- 4 bone-in skin-on chicken thighs
- 2 teaspoons olive oil
- salt and pepper to taste
- 1 small white onion, minced
- 1 ¼ cups short grain rice
- 2 ½ cups chicken broth
- ¼ cup white wine
- 1 cup chopped tomatoes
- ¼ cup basil pesto
- ¼ cup shredded Parmesan cheese

Directions:
1. Preheat the oven to 375 degrees F.
2. Heat the olive oil in a deep pan. Season the thighs with salt and pepper. Put the chicken in the pan and cook for about 5 to 6 minutes. Then turn the chicken over and cook for 5 more minutes.
3. Take the thighs from the pan and add in the chopped onions. Sauté for about 5 minutes, then stir in the rice and cook for 2 more minutes.
4. Add the wine and let it simmer until all the wine has evaporated. Pour in the broth and a dash of salt.
5. Bring the chicken back into the pan and boil the liquid. Then, cover the pan and put it in the oven. Let it bake for 40 minutes.
6. Take the chicken out of the pan. Mix the rice with pesto, tomatoes and Parmesan cheese.
7. Serve by placing the chicken on top of the rice.

Roasted Chicken, Potatoes and Peppers

Prep Time: 10 minutes; **Cook Time:** 40 minutes	
Serving Size: 637g; **Serves:** 4; **Calories:** 645	
Total Fat: 33g **Saturated Fat:** 10g; **Trans Fat:** 0g	
Protein: 48g; **Net Carbs:** 35g	
Total Carbs: 42g; **Dietary Fiber:** 7g; **Sugars:** 9.4g	
Cholesterol: 180mg; **Sodium:** 954mg; **Potassium:** 1554mg;	
Vitamin A: 203%; **Vitamin C:** 190%; **Calcium:** 6%; **Iron:** 11%.	

Ingredients:

- 3 1/3 cup potatoes, peeled and quartered
- 8 chicken thighs, skinless and boneless
- 2/3 cup diced bacon lardons
- 2 red peppers, cut into wedges
- 1 large red onion, 8 wedges
- 3 carrots, chopped
- 2 sprigs rosemary
- 1 tablespoon olive oil
- juice of 1 lemon
- 20 cherry tomatoes
- ½ cup green olives

Directions:

1. Preheat the oven to 430 degrees F.
2. Microwave the potatoes for about 5 minutes.
3. In the meantime, add the chicken, bacon, peppers, onion, carrots, rosemary and olive oil in a roasting tray. Add the microwaved potatoes and toss it all together. Sprinkle with olive oil and pop it in the oven for about half an hour.
4. After half an hour, mix the contents of the tray, add the tomatoes and olives and bake for another 15 minutes.

Creamy Risotto with Chicken

Prep Time: 10 minutes; **Cook Time:** 50 minutes	
Serving Size: 545g; **Serves:** 5; **Calories:** 751	
Total Fat: 40g **Saturated Fat:** 6.2g; **Trans Fat:** 0g	
Protein: 42.9g; **Net Carbs:** 46.1g	
Total Carbs: 47.2g; **Dietary Fiber:** 1.1g; **Sugars:** 4.4g	
Cholesterol: 185mg; **Sodium:** 1140mg; **Potassium:** 137mg;	
Vitamin A: 13%; **Vitamin C:** 8%; **Calcium:** 25%; **Iron:** 13%.	

Ingredients:
- ½ tablespoon olive oil
- lemon pepper seasoning
- 2 pounds chicken thighs, with skin and bone
- 2 tablespoons butter
- 4 garlic cloves, minced
- 1 onion, finely diced
- 1 ½ cups risotto rice
- ½ cup white wine
- 4 cups chicken broth
- 1 cup milk
- ½ tsp salt
- black pepper, to taste
- 1 tablespoon butter
- ½ cup milk
- 1 cup grated Parmesan cheese

Directions:
1. Preheat the oven to 390 degrees F.
2. Coat the chicken with lemon pepper seasoning.
3. Heat the oil in a pan, suitable for the oven.
4. Put the chicken in the pan and cook for 5 minutes on one side and 3 minutes on the other.
5. Take the chicken out on a plate. Soak all the extra oil from the pan; wipe it with a paper towel.
6. To make the risotto, place the pan back on the stove and melt the butter. Add in the garlic and onion and sauté for about 2 minutes.
7. Pour in the rice, add wine and cook for about 2 minutes, so the wine evaporates.
8. Add in the broth, milk, salt and pepper. Bring it to a simmer. Stir and then add the baked chicken on top of the risotto. Cover with a lid or tin foil. Put the pan into the oven.
9. Bake covered with the lid for 20 minutes. Uncover and bake for another 10 minutes.

10. Remove the chicken and finish the risotto by adding in the milk and butter so it's nice and creamy.
11. Sprinkle with Parmesan cheese before serving.

Chicken with Couscous

Prep Time: 20 minutes; **Cook Time:** 60 minutes
Serving Size: 640g; **Serves:** 4; **Calories:** 692
Total Fat: 38g **Saturated Fat:** 10.5g; **Trans Fat:** 0g
Protein: 46g; **Net Carbs:** 29g
Total Carbs: 32g; **Dietary Fiber:** 3g; **Sugars:** 2.7g
Cholesterol: 193mg; **Sodium:** 835mg; **Potassium:** 108mg;
Vitamin A: 12%; **Vitamin C:** 18%; **Calcium:** 7%; **Iron:** 16%.

Ingredients:
- [ ] 2 pounds chicken, with skin and bones cut into pieces
- [ ] 1 tablespoon olive oil
- [ ] 1 large red onion, coarsely chopped
- [ ] 4 garlic cloves, minced
- [ ] 2 yellow squashes, coarsely chopped
- [ ] ½ cup dry white wine
- [ ] 3 cups couscous, cooked
- [ ] 3 cups chicken stock
- [ ] 1 teaspoon garlic powder
- [ ] salt and pepper, to taste
- [ ] 1 tablespoon fresh parsley, chopped

Directions:
1. Preheat the oven to 375 degrees F.
2. Place the chicken and olive oil in a pan suitable for the oven and brown the chicken by baking it about 3 minutes per side. Remove the chicken from the pan.
3. Add the onion, minced garlic and squash in the same pan. Sauté for about 5 minutes.
4. Pour in the wine. Add the couscous, chicken stock and garlic powder. Season with salt and pepper to taste. Stir well. Put the chicken on top of the couscous and cover the pan.
5. Bake covered for 40 minutes. Remove the lid and bake for 20 more minutes.
6. Serve with fresh parsley.

Quinoa Chicken with Feta Cheese

Prep Time: 15 minutes; **Cook Time:** 55 minutes	
Serving Size: 605g; **Serves:** 6; **Calories:** 540	
Total Fat: 28g **Saturated Fat:** 7.5g; **Trans Fat:** 0g	
Protein: 29g; **Net Carbs:** 38.2g	
Total Carbs: 43g; **Dietary Fiber:** 4.8g; **Sugars:** 6.5g	
Cholesterol: 94mg; **Sodium:** 1267mg; **Potassium:** 787mg;	
Vitamin A: 18%; **Vitamin C:** 142%; **Calcium:** 19%; **Iron:** 22%.	

Ingredients:
- 1 pound boneless, skinless chicken, cubed
- 1 tablespoon olive oil
- 4 garlic cloves, minced
- ½ cup fresh basil, shredded
- juice and zest from ½ lemon
- salt and pepper, to taste
- 1 onion, diced
- 2 medium zucchini, chopped
- 1 red bell pepper, chopped
- 2 cups chicken broth
- 1 can diced tomatoes
- 1 cup quinoa, uncooked
- 1 can artichoke hearts
- ½ cup cherry tomatoes, halved
- 1 cup feta cheese, crumbled

Directions:
1. Marinate the chicken in oil, half of the minced garlic, half of the basil, lemon juice, salt and pepper.
2. When done, chop all the vegetables.
3. Preheat the oven to 350 degrees F and heat the oil in a pot that is also suitable for the oven. Add the chicken and cook for around 5 minutes. Transfer the chicken to a plate.
4. In the pan, sauté the onion and minced garlic for about 2 minutes. Toss in the zucchini and pepper and cook for another 3 or 4 minutes.
5. Pour in the broth, canned diced tomatoes and quinoa. Let it simmer.
6. Add the chicken, artichoke hearts and tomatoes.
7. Place the pot in the oven and bake for 20 minutes.
8. Cover with a lid and bake for another 20 minutes.
9. When done, sprinkle with feta cheese and serve.

Simple Chicken from the Oven

Prep Time: 10 minutes; **Cook Time:** 75 minutes	
Serving Size: 215g; **Serves:** 4; **Calories:** 373	
Total Fat: 29g **Saturated Fat:** 8.6g; **Trans Fat:** 0g	
Protein: 30g; **Net Carbs:** 3.6g	
Total Carbs: 4.3g; **Dietary Fiber:** 0.7g; **Sugars:** 1.6g	
Cholesterol: 122mg; **Sodium:** 303mg; **Potassium:** 280mg;	
Vitamin A: 7%; **Vitamin C:** 28%; **Calcium:** 2%; **Iron:** 7%.	

Ingredients:
- ☐ olive oil
- ☐ 1 sprig of rosemary
- ☐ 4 cloves of garlic, unpeeled
- ☐ 4 large chicken legs with skins on
- ☐ 5 ounces chorizo, cut into thick slices
- ☐ the juice of ½ lemon
- ☐ 8 ounces cherry tomatoes, halved

Directions:
1. Preheat the oven to 390 degrees F.
2. Drizzle a casserole with olive oil, scatter with rosemary leaves and garlic cloves. Add in the chicken. Season with some salt and pepper.
3. Place the chorizo all around the chicken and drizzle with lemon juice.
4. Place the dish in the oven and bake for about 45 minutes. Add the tomatoes and coat the chicken with olive oil. Bake for 10 to 15 minutes more.
5. When done, serve the chicken with some tomatoes and pan juice.

Baked Chicken with Potatoes

Prep Time: 15 minutes; **Cook Time:** 60 minutes
Serving Size: 400g; **Serves:** 6; **Calories:** 436
Total Fat: 23g **Saturated Fat:** 5g; **Trans Fat:** 0g
Protein: 36.5g; **Net Carbs:** 16g
Total Carbs: 18.5g; **Dietary Fiber:** 2.5g; **Sugars:** 1.3g
Cholesterol: 137mg; **Sodium:** 735mg; **Potassium:** 486mg;
Vitamin A: 9%; **Vitamin C:** 19%; **Calcium:** 8%; **Iron:** 9%.

Ingredients:

- 1 tablespoon olive oil
- 6 small chicken drumsticks
- 6 chicken thigh cutlets
- 2 pounds small potatoes, halved
- 2 ripe tomatoes, finely chopped
- 1/2 cup Kalamata olives
- 2 garlic cloves, peeled, thinly sliced
- 1/2 cup dry white wine
- salt and pepper, to taste

Directions:

1. Preheat the oven to 390 degrees F.
2. Heat the olive oil in a dish suitable for baking in the oven. Add the chicken drumsticks and cook for about 5 minutes. Remove them to a plate and cover with tin foil to retain warmth.
3. Do the same with the thigh cutlets.
4. Then, add the potatoes to the same dish and cook for about 5 minutes, until golden brown. Remove the dish from the heat. Add the chicken and top everything with tomatoes, olives and sliced garlic. Pour over the wine and season with salt and pepper.
5. Place the dish in the oven and bake for 45 minutes. Serve right away.

Chicken with Orzo Pasta

Prep Time: 15 minutes; **Cook Time:** 35 minutes	
Serving Size: 604g; **Serves:** 4; **Calories:** 601	
Total Fat: 20.3g **Saturated Fat:** 4g; **Trans Fat:** 3.5g	
Protein: 36.1g; **Net Carbs:** 61.5g	
Total Carbs: 70g; **Dietary Fiber:** 9.5g; **Sugars:** 5.4g	
Cholesterol: 94mg; **Sodium:** 1759mg; **Potassium:** 741mg;	
Vitamin A: 4%; **Vitamin C:** 19%; **Calcium:** 16%; **Iron:** 24%.	

Ingredients:
- ☐ 4 skinless bone-in chicken thighs
- ☐ 2 teaspoons olive oil
- ☐ 1 small onion, finely diced
- ☐ 2 cloves of garlic, minced
- ☐ ½ cup roasted peppers, roughly chopped
- ☐ 8 ounces whole wheat orzo pasta
- ☐ ¾ cup green olives, halved
- ☐ 1 (15-ounce) can of chickpeas, drained and rinsed
- ☐ 3 cups chicken broth
- ☐ salt and pepper, to taste

Directions:
1. Preheat the oven to 375 degrees F. Heat the olive oil in a large pot.
2. Season the chicken with salt and pepper. Place it in the pan and cook for 4 to 6 minutes per side. Transfer the chicken to a plate.
3. Add the onion to the pan and sauté for about 5 minutes. Add the minced garlic and cooked for another minute.
4. Add the pasta, roasted peppers, olives and chickpeas into the pan. Put the chicken on top of it and pour the chicken broth over it. Season to taste.
5. Bring it to a boil, cover the pot and place it into the oven. Bake for 35 minutes.
6. Serve while still warm.

Lemon Grilled Chicken

Prep Time: 5 minutes; **Cook Time:** 15 minutes
Serving Size: 183g; **Serves:** 4; **Calories:** 284
Total Fat: 22.7g **Saturated Fat:** 4.8g; **Trans Fat:** 0g
Protein: 19.8g; **Net Carbs:** 3.1g
Total Carbs: 4.3g; **Dietary Fiber:** 1.2g; **Sugars:** 1.3g
Cholesterol: 90mg; **Sodium:** 82mg; **Potassium:** 384mg;
Vitamin A: 8%; **Vitamin C:** 27%; **Calcium:** 4%; **Iron:** 5%.

Ingredients:
- ¼ cup olive oil
- 2 tablespoons lemon juice
- 1 teaspoon lemon zest
- 1 teaspoon minced garlic
- salt and pepper, to taste
- 4 chicken thighs
- 1 lemon, cut into 4 wedges
- 8 green onions

Directions:
1. Whisk together the olive oil, lemon juice, zest, minced garlic, salt and pepper. Toss in the chicken things and coat them with the mixture.
2. Heat the grill to medium and grill the chicken for about 5 to 8 minutes on the skin side, turn over and grill for about 4 minutes on the other side.
3. Grill the lemon wedges and green onion for a few minutes.
4. Serve them with the chicken.

Casseroles

Chicken Casserole with Mushrooms

Prep Time: 10 minutes; **Cook Time:** 30 minutes	
Serving Size: 335g; **Serves:** 3; **Calories:** 336	
Total Fat: 16.2g **Saturated Fat:** 0.7g; **Trans Fat:** 0g	
Protein: 18.3g; **Net Carbs:** 20.4g	
Total Carbs: 24g; **Dietary Fiber:** 3.6g; **Sugars:** 2.5g	
Cholesterol: 39mg; **Sodium:** 574mg; **Potassium:** 567mg;	
Vitamin A: 3%; **Vitamin C:** 104%; **Calcium:** 1%; **Iron:** 28%.	

Ingredients:
- 1 tablespoon olive oil
- 3-6 chicken fillets, diced
- ½ yellow onion, finely chopped
- 1 clove garlic, minced
- 4 tomatoes, diced
- 1 green pepper, sliced into 8 pieces
- ½ cup dry white wine
- 1 cup mushrooms, halved
- 6 black olives, pitted and halved

Directions:
1. Heat the olive oil on medium heat and brown the chicken pieces for about 1 minute per side.
2. Remove the chicken to a separate plate.
3. Toss the chopped onion and minced garlic into the pan and stir fry it for about 2 minutes.
4. Add the pepper and tomatoes and stir fry for about 2 more minutes.
5. Pour in the wine, mushrooms, olives and chicken. Bring everything to a simmer.
6. Cover with a lid and let it simmer for about 20 minutes.

Vegetarian Zucchini Casserole

Prep Time: 20 minutes; **Cook Time:** 40 minutes
Serving Size: 802g; **Serves:** 4; **Calories:** 411
Total Fat: 24.7g **Saturated Fat:** 10.9g; **Trans Fat:** 0g
Protein: 16.4g; **Net Carbs:** 22.5g
Total Carbs: 37.6g; **Dietary Fiber:** 15.1g; **Sugars:** 21g
Cholesterol: 134mg; **Sodium:** 470mg; **Potassium:** 1753mg;
Vitamin A: 61%; **Vitamin C:** 116%; **Calcium:** 41%; **Iron:** 13%.

Ingredients:

- 2 medium zucchini, sliced
- 2 medium eggplant, peeled and sliced
- 2 medium red onion, sliced
- 6 medium tomatoes, sliced
- 3 cloves of garlic, minced
- 2 eggs
- 1 cup grated Parmesan cheese
- ¾ cup sour cream
- 2 tablespoons olive oil
- 1 ½ teaspoons oregano
- 1 ½ teaspoons basil
- salt and pepper, to taste

Directions:

1. Preheat the oven to 340 degrees F.
2. Grease a dish suitable for the oven with olive oil.
3. Layer the eggplant slices on the bottom of the dish, season with salt and pepper, layer the onion slices on top of that, then zucchini slices, season again, and finish off with a layer of tomato slices. Sprinkle with half the oregano and basil, then sprinkle with Parmesan cheese.
4. Repeat the layers until you run out of vegetables.
5. In a medium bowl, mic the minced garlic, sour cream and eggs. Season with the remaining oregano and basil. Pour this mixture on top of the assembled vegetables.
6. Sprinkle the top with some more cheese,
7. Bake for about 30 minutes, until the top is golden brown.

Rigatoni and Cheese Casserole

Prep Time: 20 minutes; **Cook Time:** 40 minutes	
Serving Size: 328g; **Serves:** 8; **Calories:** 463	
Total Fat: 15.8g **Saturated Fat:** 5.8g; **Trans Fat:** 0g	
Protein: 21.1g; **Net Carbs:** 54.6g	
Total Carbs: 61.9g; **Dietary Fiber:** 7.3g; **Sugars:** 12g	
Cholesterol: 27mg; **Sodium:** 523mg; **Potassium:** 615mg;	
Vitamin A: 22%; **Vitamin C:** 36%; **Calcium:** 24%; **Iron:** 29%.	

Ingredients:

- 1 pound rigatoni pasta, dry
- ¼ cup olive oil, divided
- 2 cups chopped brown mushrooms
- 2 cups sliced sweet onion
- 1 pound zucchini, diced
- 6 cloves garlic, minced
- 6 scallions, sliced
- ¼ cup kalamata olives, halved
- ¼ teaspoon dried oregano
- ¼ teaspoon dried thyme
- 1 teaspoon salt
- 1 (28-ounce) can crushed tomatoes, undrained
- 8 ounces mozzarella cheese, shredded
- 2 ounces Parmesan cheese, grated

Directions:

1. Preheat the oven to 350 degrees F. Cook the pasta according to package directions. Drain and set aside.
2. Heat 2 teaspoons of olive oil in a skillet, toss in the mushrooms and sauté for about 2 minutes. Remove them from skillet and set aside.
3. Pour another 2 teaspoons of olive oil to skillet, toss in the onion and sauté for 5 minutes. Add the chopped zucchini and sauté for 3 more minutes. Toss in the garlic, scallions, olives, oregano, thyme and salt. Sauté for another 30 seconds.
4. Add the crushed tomatoes and bring the mixture to a boil. Cover with a lid and let it simmer for 15 minutes. Add in the mushrooms and stir well.
5. Combine the cooked pasta and tomato sauce to a 13 x 9 - inch baking dish. Add the mozzarella and stir everything well. Sprinkle Parmesan cheese. Cover the dish with tin foil and bake for 15 minutes. Uncover and bake for another 5 minutes.
6. Let it cool for 15 minutes before serving.

Egg Casserole with Artichokes

Prep Time: 15 minutes; **Cook Time:** 35 minutes	
Serving Size: 218g; **Serves:** 6; **Calories:** 320	
Total Fat: 18.g **Saturated Fat:** 9.7g; **Trans Fat:** 0g	
Protein: 19.6g; **Net Carbs:** 14.2g	
Total Carbs: 19.5g; **Dietary Fiber:** 5.3g; **Sugars:** 3.4g	
Cholesterol: 229mg; **Sodium:** 809mg; **Potassium:** 303mg;	
Vitamin A: 38%; **Vitamin C:** 31%; **Calcium:** 26%; **Iron:** 13%.	

Ingredients:

- 10 ounces frozen artichokes, thawed
- 1 large tomato, chopped
- 1 shallot, chopped
- 1 cup fresh parsley leaves, roughly chopped
- 1 cup fresh mint leaves, roughly chopped
- 1 ¼ cup crumbled feta cheese
- ½ cup ground Parmesan cheese
- 6 slices fresh toast, cut into ½-inch pieces
- 1 cup milk
- ¾ cup heavy cream
- 6 eggs
- ½ tsp baking powder
- salt and pepper, to taste

Directions:

1. Preheat the oven to 375 degrees F.
2. Chop the artichokes and mix them with chopped tomato, shallot, parsley, mint leaves, feta and Parmesan cheese. Set the mixture aside.
3. Cut the 6 slices of toast, chop them into ½-inch pieces and toss them in a large bowl. Set aside.
4. In a medium bowl, whisk together the milk, heavy cream, eggs, baking powder, salt and pepper to taste.
5. Pour this egg mixture into the bowl with bread and mix in the vegetables and cheeses. Stir very well.
6. Transfer the mixture into a baking dish and bake in the oven for about 35 minutes.

Glazed Chicken Casserole

Prep Time: 10 minutes; **Cook Time:** 20 minutes

Serving Size: 346g; **Serves:** 6; **Calories:** 473

Total Fat: 22.8g **Saturated Fat:** 6.4g; **Trans Fat:** 0g

Protein: 39g; **Net Carbs:** 22g

Total Carbs: 28.5g; **Dietary Fiber:** 6.5g; **Sugars:** 6.2g

Cholesterol: 90mg; **Sodium:** 452mg; **Potassium:** 582mg;

Vitamin A: 9%; **Vitamin C:** 20%; **Calcium:** 32%; **Iron:** 27%.

Ingredients:
- ½ cup balsamic vinegar
- 1 tablespoon olive oil
- 6 boneless skinless chicken breasts
- salt and pepper, to taste
- 1 (14-ounce) can of marinated artichoke hearts
- ½ red onion, thinly sliced
- 1 cup cherry tomatoes, left whole
- 1 (14-ounce) can white beans, drained and rinsed
- ¾ cup whole salted cashews
- 1 ½ cup chicken broth
- 1 cup shredded mozzarella

Directions:
1. Marinate the chicken breasts in balsamic vinegar for at least 30 minutes.
2. Meanwhile, preheat the oven to 400 degrees F.
3. In a large casserole dish, mix the white beans, cashews, cherry tomatoes, artichoke hearts, and onion slices.
4. Season the chicken with salt and pepper, heat the olive oil in skillet and cook the chicken for about 2 minutes per side.
5. Place the chicken into the casserole, on top of the vegetables.
6. Pour in the chicken broth and let it cook in the oven for 15 to 20 minutes.
7. After you remove it from the oven, sprinkle the casserole with fresh shredded mozzarella.

Kale Quinoa Casserole

Prep Time: 15 minutes; **Cook Time:** 35 minutes	
Serving Size: 180g; **Serves:** 6; **Calories:** 331	
Total Fat: 18.7g **Saturated Fat:** 8.5g; **Trans Fat:** 0g	
Protein: 18g; **Net Carbs:** 19g	
Total Carbs: 22g; **Dietary Fiber:** 3g; **Sugars:** 7.3g	
Cholesterol: 40mg; **Sodium:** 875mg; **Potassium:** 236mg;	
Vitamin A: 34%; **Vitamin C:** 20%; **Calcium:** 31%; **Iron:** 21%.	

Ingredients:
- 1 cup fresh kale, chopped
- 2 1/2 cups mozzarella cheese, shredded
- 1 cup sun-dried tomatoes packed in oil, chopped
- 1/2 cup pitted black olives, sliced
- 1 cup cooked quinoa
- 5 cooked Italian sausages, chopped
- 1 1/2 cups pasta sauce
- 2 teaspoon garlic powder
- pinch of salt and black pepper
- 1/4 cup Parmesan cheese, grated
- 1/4 cup bread crumbs

Directions:
1. Preheat the oven to 375 degrees F. Grease a 9 x 13 baking dish.
2. Toss all the ingredients except for the cheese and bread crumbs in the dish and stir well.
3. Sprinkle the mixture with Parmesan cheese and bread crumbs.
4. Bake for 25 to 30 minutes, so the top gets nice and crispy.

Rice and Bean Casserole

Prep Time: 5 minutes; **Cook Time:** 35 minutes	
Serving Size: 148g; **Serves:** 4; **Calories:** 214	
Total Fat: 9.2g **Saturated Fat:** 1g; **Trans Fat:** 0g	
Protein: 5.4g; **Net Carbs:** 23.8g	
Total Carbs: 28.2g; **Dietary Fiber:** 4.4g; **Sugars:** 9.2g	
Cholesterol: 0mg; **Sodium:** 86mg; **Potassium:** 409mg;	
Vitamin A: 34%; **Vitamin C:** 19%; **Calcium:** 4%; **Iron:** 13%.	

Ingredients:

- [ ] 1 tablespoon olive oil
- [ ] 1 cup cooked brown rice
- [ ] ½ can kidney beans, drained and rinsed
- [ ] ¼ cup toasted pine nuts
- [ ] ¼ cup raisins
- [ ] ½ large red onion, diced
- [ ] 2 cloves garlic, minced
- [ ] ¼ cup parsley, chopped
- [ ] ½ lemon, juiced
- [ ] 2 cups baby spinach
- [ ] 1 tsp dried thyme
- [ ] ¼ tsp paprika
- [ ] salt and pepper, to taste

Directions:

1. Preheat the oven to 350 degrees F.
2. In a large pot, heat the olive oil, toss in the onions and garlic and sauté for about 10 minutes.
3. Add all the remaining ingredients except for the cooked rice and stir well.
4. Reduce the heat, cover with a lid and let it simmer for 5 minutes.
5. Stir in the cooked rice.
6. Transfer everything to a casserole and bake for about 20 minutes.

Fish

Lemon Orzo Shrimp

Prep Time: 10 minutes; **Cook Time:** 30 minutes	
Serving Size: 440g; **Serves:** 4; **Calories:** 406	
Total Fat: 7g **Saturated Fat:** 1.2g; **Trans Fat:** 0g	
Protein: 35g; **Net Carbs:** 48g	
Total Carbs: 53g; **Dietary Fiber:** 5g; **Sugars:** 8g	
Cholesterol: 226mg; **Sodium:** 975mg; **Potassium:** 66mg;	
Vitamin A: 17%; **Vitamin C:** 19%; **Calcium:** 10%; **Iron:** 34%.	

Ingredients:
- 1 pound medium shrimp, peeled and deveined
- salt and pepper, to taste
- 1 tablespoon olive oil
- 3 cloves garlic, minced
- 1 onion, diced
- 8 ounces orzo pasta
- 2 cups chicken broth
- 1 (14.5-ounce) can diced tomatoes, drained
- 1/2 cup frozen peas
- juice of 1 lemon
- ¼ cup grated Parmesan cheese

Directions:
1. Preheat the oven to 400 degrees F and season the shrimp.
2. Heat the olive oil in a skillet, add the garlic and onion and sauté for 3 to 4 minutes.
3. Stir in the pasta and cook for 1 to 3 minutes more.
4. Pour in the broth and water. Bring to a boil, reduce the heat, cover with a lid and let it simmer for about 10 minutes.
5. When done, add the tomatoes, peas, lemon juice and shrimp. Sprinkle it with Parmesan cheese.
6. Place the dish in the oven and bake for 12 to 14 minutes.

Microwave Fish with Green Beans

Prep Time: 8 minutes; **Cook Time:** 8 minutes

Serving Size: 281g; **Serves:** 2; **Calories:** 235

Total Fat: 11.1g **Saturated Fat:** 2.1g; **Trans Fat:** 0g

Protein: 24.6g; **Net Carbs:** 7.3g

Total Carbs: 11.4g; **Dietary Fiber:** 4.1g; **Sugars:** 3.2g

Cholesterol: 50mg; **Sodium:** 993mg; **Potassium:** 484mg;

Vitamin A: 22%; **Vitamin C:** 41%; **Calcium:** 8%; **Iron:** 11%.

Ingredients:

- ½ pound green beans, trimmed
- ½ cup cherry tomatoes, halved
- 1 ounce Kalamata olives, sliced
- 2 garlic cloves, minced
- 1 tablespoon olive oil
- ¾ teaspoon salt
- 2 (6-ounce) tilapia fillets, ½ inch thick

Directions:

1. Add the green beans, cherry tomatoes, olives, garlic, olive oil and salt in a dish, suitable for the microwave. Cover with a plastic wrap and poke a hole in the middle, to let the air out. Microwave on high for 3 minutes.
2. Remove from the microwave and stir well.
3. Add the fillets on top of the greens, cover with the plastic wrap again and microwave for another 2 ½ minutes.
4. If the fish is still not done, microwave for another 20 seconds.
5. Before serving, let the dish sit covered for about 2 more minutes.

Roasted Salmon with Rice

Prep Time: 10 minutes; **Cook Time:** 40 minutes
Serving Size: 470g; **Serves:** 4; **Calories:** 572
Total Fat: 21g **Saturated Fat:** 4.3g; **Trans Fat:** 0g
Protein: 49g; **Net Carbs:** 40g
Total Carbs: 46g; **Dietary Fiber:** 6g; **Sugars:** 1g
Cholesterol: 36mg; **Sodium:** 588mg; **Potassium:** 541mg;
Vitamin A: 77%; **Vitamin C:** 44%; **Calcium:** 6%; **Iron:** 13%.

Ingredients:

- 2 cups chicken broth
- 1 cup long-grain white rice
- 5 ounces fresh spinach
- 1 jar marinated artichokes, drained
- 2 garlic cloves, minced
- 1 cup grape tomatoes, halved
- 1/2 cup black olives, sliced
- 4 small salmon fillets
- 2 tablespoons olive oil
- 2 tablespoons lemon juice
- salt to taste

Directions:

1. Preheat the oven to 400 degrees F and boil the broth in a pan suitable for the oven. Add the rice.
2. Top with the spinach, artichokes and garlic. Place the tomatoes and olives around the edge of the dish. Spread the salmon on top of the spinach mixture, sprinkle with oil, lemon juice and salt. Seal tightly with aluminum foil.
3. Bake for 30 minutes, take off the foil and continue baking for 5 to 7 minutes.
4. Serve while still warm.

Quick and Easy Baked Fish

Prep Time: 15 minutes; **Cook Time:** 15 minutes
Serving Size: 330g; **Serves:** 4; **Calories:** 179
Total Fat: 6g **Saturated Fat:** 1.5g; **Trans Fat:** 0g
Protein: 24g; **Net Carbs:** 6g
Total Carbs: 8.5g; **Dietary Fiber:** 2.5g; **Sugars:** 4.8g
Cholesterol: 50mg; **Sodium:** 664mg; **Potassium:** 676mg;
Vitamin A: 10%; **Vitamin C:** 36%; **Calcium:** 6%; **Iron:** 8%.

Ingredients:
- 1 tablespoon olive oil
- 1 large onion, diced
- 1 can diced tomatoes
- 1 teaspoon oregano
- 1 teaspoon basil
- 4 boneless, skinless fish fillets (cod or tilapia)
- 2 tablespoons capers, drained
- salt and pepper, to taste

Directions:
1. Preheat the oven to 375 degrees F.
2. Heat the olive oil in a large pan, suitable for the oven.
3. Add the onion and sauté for about 8 minutes.
4. Add the tomatoes, oregano, basil and capers. Stir on medium heat for about 5 minutes.
5. Add the fish fillets.
6. Place the dish in the oven and bake for around 15 minutes. Make sure to check the fish frequently, as its cooking time depends on its size.
7. Serve immediately.

Baked Tilapia with Feta Cheese

Prep Time: 5 minutes; **Cook Time:** 15 minutes	
Serving Size: 154g; **Serves:** 4; **Calories:** 213	
Total Fat: 12g **Saturated Fat:** 5.4g; **Trans Fat:** 0g	
Protein: 23.4g; **Net Carbs:** 1.3g	
Total Carbs: 1.7g; **Dietary Fiber:** 0.4g; **Sugars:** 0.6g	
Cholesterol: 70mg; **Sodium:** 602mg; **Potassium:** 340++52mg;	
Vitamin A: 6%; **Vitamin C:** 19%; **Calcium:** 4%; **Iron:** 4%.	

Ingredients:
- 4 tilapia fillets
- 2 tablespoons butter, melted
- 1/4 cup lemon juice
- salt and pepper, to taste
- 4 lemon slices
- 1/4 cup red bell pepper, chopped
- 1/4 cup black olives, sliced
- 1/4 cup feta cheese, crumbled

Directions:
1. Heat the oven to 425 degrees F. Grease a 9 x 12-inch baking pan with oil.
2. Brush the tilapia fillets with melted butter and drizzle lemon juice over them. Season them with salt and pepper.
3. Top with chopped pepper, olives and one lemon slice each.
4. Place it in the oven and bake for around 15 minutes.
5. When done, sprinkle with feta cheese and serve immediately.

Swordfish with Tomatoes

Prep Time: 5 minutes; **Cook Time:** 30 minutes	
Serving Size: 368g; **Serves:** 4; **Calories:** 408	
Total Fat: 14.5g **Saturated Fat:** 3.1g; **Trans Fat:** 0g	
Protein: 57.5g; **Net Carbs:** 4.1g	
Total Carbs: 5.3g; **Dietary Fiber:** 1.2g; **Sugars:** 2.8g	
Cholesterol: 107mg; **Sodium:** 824mg; **Potassium:** 67mg;	
Vitamin A: 21%; **Vitamin C:** 23%; **Calcium:** 2%; **Iron:** 16%.	

Ingredients:
- 1 medium onion, chopped
- 2 teaspoons olive oil
- 1 garlic clove, minced
- ½ teaspoon salt, divided
- ½ cup chicken broth
- ¼ cup chopped pimiento-stuffed olives
- 1 tablespoon small capers, drained
- 4 (8-ounce) swordfish steaks
- 2 plum tomatoes, seeded and diced

Directions:
1. Heat the olive oil in a skillet, add the chopped onion and sauté for about 3 minutes. Add the garlic and salt and sauté for another minute. Pour in the chicken broth, olives and capers. Reduce the heat.
2. Place the fillets on top of the vegetables. Cover with a lid and bake for 26 minutes.
3. Serve with fresh diced tomatoes.

Fish Stew with Prawns

Prep Time: 5 minutes; **Cook Time:** 35 minutes

Serving Size: 365g; **Serves:** 4; **Calories:** 250

Total Fat: 8.2g **Saturated Fat:** 1.1g; **Trans Fat:** 0g

Protein: 30.4g; **Net Carbs:** 4.9g

Total Carbs: 7.2g; **Dietary Fiber:** 2.3g; **Sugars:** 0.5g

Cholesterol: 0mg; **Sodium:** 303mg; **Potassium:** 401mg;

Vitamin A: 5%; **Vitamin C:** 15%; **Calcium:** 4%; **Iron:** 6%.

Ingredients:
- 2 tablespoons olive oil
- 2 cloves garlic, slivered
- fennel bulb, halved and shredded
- ½ cup white wine
- 1 (14-ounce) can tomatoes
- 1 ¼ cup chicken stock
- 15 ounces firm white fish, cut into chunks
- 9 ounces cooked peeled prawns

Directions:
1. Heat the olive oil in a large pan. Add garlic and sauté for 2 minutes. Add the fennel and cook for another 5 minutes. Then pour in the wine and let it simmer until the wine evaporates.
2. Add the tomatoes and chicken stock. Let it simmer for 15 to 20 minutes Add the white fish, cover with a lid and cook for 3 more minutes.
3. Finish off by adding the cooked prawns and let it simmer for a couple of minutes more, until heated through.

Salmon with Vegetable Quinoa

Prep Time: 10 minutes; **Cook Time:** 20 minutes	
Serving Size: 225g; **Serves:** 4; **Calories:** 367	
Total Fat: 11.6g **Saturated Fat:** 1.7g; **Trans Fat:** 0g	
Protein: 34.5g; **Net Carbs:** 26.6g	
Total Carbs: 29.9g; **Dietary Fiber:** 3.6g; **Sugars:** 1.1g	
Cholesterol: 78mg; **Sodium:** 65mg; **Potassium:** 993mg;	
Vitamin A: 2%; **Vitamin C:** 15%; **Calcium:** 4%; **Iron:** 18%.	

Ingredients:
- 1 cup quinoa, uncooked
- Salt, to taste
- ¾ cup cucumbers, diced
- 1 cup cherry tomatoes, halved
- ¼ cup red onion, finely diced
- 4 basil leaves, thinly sliced
- zest of one lemon
- 1 teaspoon cumin
- ½ teaspoon paprika
- 20 ounces salmon fillets
- 8 lemon wedges

Directions:
1. Bring 1 cup of quinoa, 2 cups of water and some salt to a boil. Cover with a lid and let it simmer for about 20 minutes. Remove from the stove and let it sit for 5 more minutes.
2. Right before serving, toss in the cucumbers, tomatoes, onions, basil and lemon zest. In the meantime, prepare the salmon.
3. Mix some salt, cumin and paprika in a small bowl.
4. Transfer the salmon fillets to a greased dish and coat them with the spices. Cover with lemon wedges and broil the salmon on high for 8 to 10 minutes.
5. Serve the salmon with the lemon wedges and quinoa.

Baked Halibut with Artichokes

Prep Time: 15 minutes; **Cook Time:** 15 minutes

Serving Size: 428g; **Serves:** 4; **Calories:** 356

Total Fat: 18g **Saturated Fat:** 2.7g; **Trans Fat:** 0g

Protein: 34.4g; **Net Carbs:** 13g

Total Carbs: 20.3g; **Dietary Fiber:** 7.3g; **Sugars:** 6.9g

Cholesterol: 45mg; **Sodium:** 1609mg; **Potassium:** 1307mg;

Vitamin A: 8%; **Vitamin C:** 32%; **Calcium:** 6%; **Iron:** 8%.

Ingredients:
- 4 halibut fillets
- 4 tablespoons olive oil
- 2 cups fresh salsa
- 2 cups artichoke hearts
- 1 medium red onion, sliced thin
- 8 tablespoons capers
- 8 slices lemon
- salt and pepper, to taste

Directions:

1. Preheat the oven to 400 degrees F and grease a baking dish with olive oil.
2. Season the fillets with salt and pepper and place them in the dish
3. Spoon the salsa on top of each fillet and top each one with 2 lemon slices.
4. Arrange the artichokes and onion slices around the fish. Sprinkle everything with capers.
5. Cover the dish with tin foil and bake for 14 to 16 minutes.

Tilapia with Vegetables

Prep Time: 10 minutes; **Cook Time:** 20 minutes	
Serving Size: 483g; **Serves:** 2; **Calories:** 322	
Total Fat: 9.1g **Saturated Fat:** 2.9g; **Trans Fat:** 0g	
Protein: 47.7g; **Net Carbs:** 10g	
Total Carbs: 14g; **Dietary Fiber:** 4g; **Sugars:** 6.5g	
Cholesterol: 100mg; **Sodium:** 689mg; **Potassium:** 1290mg;	
Vitamin A: 19%; **Vitamin C:** 107%; **Calcium:** 8%; **Iron:** 13%.	

Ingredients:
- 1 ½ cups grape tomatoes, halved
- 1 ½ cups zucchini, diced
- 1 cup red onion, sliced thinly
- 3 garlic cloves, minced
- ½ cup black olives, chopped
- ½ tablespoon olive oil
- juice of 2 lemons
- 1 tablespoon fresh oregano, chopped
- 1 tablespoon fresh thyme, chopped
- 4 tilapia fillets

Directions:
1. Preheat the oven to 425 degrees F.
2. Toss together the tomatoes, zucchini, onion slices, black olives, olive oil, lemon juice, oregano and thyme in a large bowl.
3. Lay two sheets of tin foil on top of each other four times.
4. Place one fish fillet in the center of one foil square and top it with ¼ of the vegetable mixture. Seal the individual packages.
5. Place them directly on the oven rack and bake for about 20 minutes.
6. Serve in the individual packages.

Pappardelle with Red Mullet

Prep Time: 5 minutes; **Cook Time:** 25 minutes	
Serving Size: 357g; **Serves:** 5; **Calories:** 503	
Total Fat: 16.1g **Saturated Fat:** 3.2g; **Trans Fat:** 0g	
Protein: 35.8g; **Net Carbs:** 46.7g	
Total Carbs: 49.7g; **Dietary Fiber:** 3g; **Sugars:** 1.8g	
Cholesterol: 117mg; **Sodium:** 230mg; **Potassium:** 765mg;	
Vitamin A: 11%; **Vitamin C:** 33%; **Calcium:** 5%; **Iron:** 33%.	

Ingredients:
- 8 shallots, finely diced
- 2 tablespoons olive oil
- 1 ounce butter
- 3 garlic cloves, crushed
- 1 ½ tablespoon harissa paste
- salt and pepper, to taste
- 6 red mullet fillets, skin on, cut into 1-inch pieces
- 3/8 cup white wine
- 2/3 cup fish stock
- 4 medium tomatoes, peeled and roughly chopped
- 3 ounces Kalamata olives, halved
- 9 ounces pappardelle pasta, dry

Directions:
1. Put the diced shallots, olive oil and butter in a large skillet and sauté for 5 minutes.
2. Add the garlic and cook for another 5 minutes.
3. Stir in the harissa paste and salt to taste. Cook for 2 minutes more.
4. Finally, add the fish fillets and cook for 2 to 3 minutes. Transfer everything to a separate bowl and set aside.
5. Pour the wine in the same skillet and let it simmer until half of it evaporates. Then pour in the fish stock and bring everything to a boil. Toss in the tomatoes, olives, salt and pepper to taste. Let it simmer 5 five minutes, so the sauce thickens.
6. In the meantime, cook the pasta according to package instructions. Drain and pour over the tomato sauce. Gently stir.
7. Finish off by gently folding in the fish mixture. Serve right away.

Sardine Escabeche

Prep Time: 10 minutes; **Cook Time:** 15 minutes

Serving Size: 213g; **Serves:** 4; **Calories:** 329

Total Fat: 22.5g **Saturated Fat:** 4.5g; **Trans Fat:** 0g

Protein: 22.9g; **Net Carbs:** 8g

Total Carbs: 10.3g; **Dietary Fiber:** 2.3g; **Sugars:** 4.5g

Cholesterol: 115mg; **Sodium:** 307mg; **Potassium:** 246mg;

Vitamin A: 208%; **Vitamin C:** 10%; **Calcium:** 33%; **Iron:** 12%.

Ingredients:
- 3 tablespoons olive oil
- 2 small onions, thinly sliced
- 4 medium carrots, peeled and thinly sliced
- 1/6 cup white wine vinegar
- 4 fresh sardines, gutted
- salt and pepper, to taste

Directions:
1. Add the olive oil and onions in a skillet and sauté for about 3 minutes.
2. Toss in the carrots, season with salt and pepper and sauté for another 5 minutes.
3. Pour in the vinegar and cook for another 2 minutes. Remove from heat.
4. Heat 1 tablespoon of oil in another pan, season the sardines and fry them in a pan for about 2 minutes per side.
5. Serve the sardines on top of the carrot sauce.

Halibut Fillets with Fennel

Prep Time: 5 minutes; **Cook Time:** 25 minutes	
Serving Size: 413g; **Serves:** 4; **Calories:** 341	
Total Fat: 12g **Saturated Fat:** 1.5g; **Trans Fat:** 0g	
Protein: 35.8g; **Net Carbs:** 16.6g	
Total Carbs: 24.4g; **Dietary Fiber:** 7.8g; **Sugars:** 4.3g	
Cholesterol: 45mg; **Sodium:** 825mg; **Potassium:** 1141mg;	
Vitamin A: 10%; **Vitamin C**: 26%; **Calcium**: 12%; **Iron**: 11%.	

Ingredients:
- 2 tablespoons olive oil, divided
- 4 halibut fillets
- ½ teaspoon salt, divided
- 1 fennel bulb, trimmed and cut into wedges
- 2 garlic cloves, minced
- 1 (14.5-ounce) can diced tomatoes
- ½ cup water
- 1 (14.5-ounce) can chickpeas, drained and rinsed

Directions:
1. Heat 1 tablespoon of olive oil in a pan over medium heat. Rub the halibut with half the salt and bake it in the pan on one side only, for 3 to 4 minutes. When done, remove to a plate.
2. Pour the remaining olive oil in the same pan and add in the fennel. Cook, while continuously stirring, for about 8 minutes. Toss in the minced garlic and cook for another minute.
3. Add in the tomatoes, water, chickpeas and the remaining salt. Bring everything to a boil, reduce the heat and let it simmer.
4. Place the halibut fillets back in, baked side up, and simmer for about 5 to 10 minutes more, until the fish is thoroughly cooked.

Simple Mediterranean Cod

Prep Time: 10 minutes; **Cook Time:** 30 minutes	
Serving Size: 245g; **Serves:** 4; **Calories:** 188	
Total Fat: 9.3g **Saturated Fat:** 1g; **Trans Fat:** 0g	
Protein: 21.1g; **Net Carbs:** 4.3g	
Total Carbs: 5.7g; **Dietary Fiber:** 1.4g; **Sugars:** 0g	
Cholesterol: 0mg; **Sodium:** 81mg; **Potassium:** 273mg;	
Vitamin A: 0%; **Vitamin C:** 35%; **Calcium:** 0%; **Iron:** 17%.	

Ingredients:
- 4 cod fillets (1/2-inch thick)
- salt and pepper, to taste
- 2 tablespoons olive oil, divided
- 4 medium tomatoes, diced
- ¼ cup sliced black olives
- 1 teaspoon dried basil

Directions:
1. Season the fillets with salt and pepper.
2. Heat 1 tablespoon of olive oil in a skillet, add the fillets and cook for about 15 seconds per side.
3. Cover the fillets with the diced tomatoes, sliced olives and basil. Reduce the heat and let it cook for about 2 minutes. Add the remaining 1 tablespoon of olive oil, cover with a lid and let it cook for another 2 minutes, until the fillets become completely opaque.

Simple Mediterranean Salmon

Prep Time: 8 minutes; **Cook Time:** 22 minutes
Serving Size: 403g; **Serves:** 4; **Calories:** 448
Total Fat: 16.9g **Saturated Fat:** 2.3g; **Trans Fat:** 0g
Protein: 64.6g; **Net Carbs:** 4.4g
Total Carbs: 5.6g; **Dietary Fiber:** 1.2g; **Sugars:** 3.3g
Cholesterol: 166mg; **Sodium:** 606mg; **Potassium:** 1068mg;
Vitamin A: 19%; **Vitamin C:** 50%; **Calcium:** 6%; **Iron:** 19%.

Ingredients:
- salt and pepper, to taste
- 4 (6-ounce) skinless salmon fillets
- olive oil, for greasing
- 2 cups cherry tomatoes, halved
- ½ cup finely chopped zucchini
- 2 tablespoons capers, undrained
- 1 tablespoon olive oil
- 2 ounces green olives, sliced

Directions:
1. Preheat the oven to 425 degrees F.
2. Season the fillets with salt and pepper. Grease a baking dish with olive oil and place the fillets in the dish in a single layer.
3. In a medium bowl, mix together the tomatoes, zucchini, capers, olive oil and green olives. Toss this mixture over the salmon fillets and bake for 22 minutes.

Baked Salmon in Tin Foil

Prep Time: 10 minutes; **Cook Time:** 20 minutes

Serving Size: 480g; **Serves:** 2; **Calories:** 511

Total Fat: 15.6g **Saturated Fat:** 4.1g; **Trans Fat:** 0g

Protein: 71.4g; **Net Carbs:** 13.4g

Total Carbs: 17.9g; **Dietary Fiber:** 4.5g; **Sugars:** 4.5g

Cholesterol: 181mg; **Sodium:** 677mg; **Potassium:** 1527mg;

Vitamin A: 22%; **Vitamin C:** 37%; **Calcium:** 18%; **Iron:** 21%.

Ingredients:
- olive oil, for greasing
- 2 4-ounce boneless salmon fillets
- salt and pepper, to taste
- 1 clove garlic, minced
- ¾ cup grape tomatoes, halved
- ¾ cup diced zucchini
- ½ cup cooked or canned chickpeas, drained
- ¼ cup chopped yellow onion
- 2 tablespoons crumbled feta cheese
- 1 tablespoon chopped fresh basil

Directions:
1. Preheat the oven to 425 degrees F. Cut 2 14-inch squares of foil and grease them with olive oil. Place 1 salmon fillet into each of them. Season with salt and pepper.
2. In a separate bowl, mix together the minced garlic, grape tomatoes, diced zucchini, chickpeas and onion. Spread the mixture evenly over the salmon.
3. Close the tin foil packages, seal tightly and transfer them to a baking sheet. Bake for 15 minutes.
4. Remove from the oven and let them sit for about 5 minutes before continuing.
5. Serve the salmon still inside the tin foil packages, sprinkled with feta cheese and fresh basil.

Oven Baked Trout

Prep Time: 5 minutes; **Cook Time:** 20 minutes	
Serving Size: 109g; **Serves:** 2; **Calories:** 312	
Total Fat: 26.3g **Saturated Fat:** 4.5g; **Trans Fat:** 0g	
Protein: 17.7g; **Net Carbs:** 2.3g	
Total Carbs: 2.3g; **Dietary Fiber:** 0g; **Sugars:** 1.5g	
Cholesterol: 48mg; **Sodium:** 30mg; **Potassium:** 313mg;	
Vitamin A: 4%; **Vitamin C:** 4%; **Calcium:** 6%; **Iron:** 1%.	

Ingredients:
- 1 large whole trout, gutted and scaled
- 3 slices blood orange
- 3-4 large sprigs of fresh fennel fronds
- 2 sprigs of fresh tarragon
- 3 tablespoons olive oil

Directions:
1. Preheat the oven to 425 degrees F.
2. Rinse the trout under cold water and dry thoroughly. Stuff the trout with the fennel fronds, tarragon and slices of blood orange.
3. Heat the olive oil in a skillet that is also suitable for the oven and toss in the trout. Bake for about 4 to 5 minutes, until the skin becomes crispy. Carefully flip it over and bake for another 4 to 5 minutes on the other side as well.
4. Transfer the skillet in the oven and bake for about 8 to 12 minutes.

Oven Baked Halibut

Prep Time: 10 minutes; **Cook Time:** 20 minutes

Serving Size: 472g; **Serves:** 4; **Calories:** 509

Total Fat: 29.6g **Saturated Fat:** 3.8g; **Trans Fat:** 0g

Protein: 49.7g; **Net Carbs:** 10.4g

Total Carbs: 15.8g; **Dietary Fiber:** 5.4g; **Sugars:** 6g

Cholesterol: 70mg; **Sodium:** 145mg; **Potassium:** 304mg;

Vitamin A: 30%; **Vitamin C:** 94%; **Calcium:** 14%; **Iron:** 19%.

Ingredients:
- juice and zest of 2 lemons
- ½ cup olive oil
- 3 cloves garlic, minced
- 2 teaspoons dill weed
- salt and pepper, to taste
- 1 tsp dried oregano
- 1 pound fresh green beans
- 1 pound cherry tomatoes
- 1 large yellow onion, sliced
- 1 ½ pounds halibut fillet, sliced into 1 ½-inch strips

Directions:
1. Preheat the oven to 450 degrees F.
2. Mix together the juice and zest of 2 lemons, olive oil minced garlic, dill, salt, pepper and oregano in a medium bowl.
3. Stir in the green beans, cherry tomatoes and onions and make sure it coats with the sauce.
4. Transfer these vegetables to one side of a large baking sheet and spread them out evenly into one layer.
5. Place the fish fillets to the other side of the sheet and sprinkle them lightly with salt.
6. Bake in the oven for about 15 minutes, transfer the sheet to the top rack and broil for 3 to 5 minutes, until the cherry tomatoes begin to pop.
7. Serve right away.

Oven Baked Branzino

Prep Time: 10 minutes; **Cook Time:** 15 minutes
Serving Size: 73g; **Serves:** 4; **Calories:** 246
Total Fat: 9.6g **Saturated Fat:** 2g; **Trans Fat:** 0g
Protein: 0.5g; **Net Carbs:** 5.3g
Total Carbs: 5.8g; **Dietary Fiber:** 0.5g; **Sugars:** 0.4g
Cholesterol: 0mg; **Sodium:** 546mg; **Potassium:** 38mg;
Vitamin A: 0%; **Vitamin C:** 15%; **Calcium:** 1%; **Iron:** 1%.

Ingredients:
- 2 whole branzino, cleaned, with head and tail intact
- 1 tablespoon olive oil
- ½ teaspoon salt
- ½ teaspoon black pepper
- 1 lemon, sliced
- 6 cloves garlic, minced

Directions:
1. Preheat the oven to 400 degrees F.
2. Rinse the fish, pat it dry and place it on a lightly oiled baking sheet.
3. Brush the fish inside and out with olive oil and season it with salt and pepper.
4. Stuff the cavities with 2 to 3 lemon slices and spread the minced garlic inside and over the fish.
5. Bake for about 5 minutes. Then, turn the fish over and bake for another 5 minutes.
6. Turn the oven to broil and broil the fish for another 3 to 5 minutes, until it flakes effortlessly with a fork.
7. Drizzle with some extra olive oil before serving.

Trout with Olives and Fennel

Prep Time: 10 minutes; **Cook Time:** 20 minutes	
Serving Size: 323g; **Serves:** 2; **Calories:** 369	
Total Fat: 21.9g **Saturated Fat:** 3.8g; **Trans Fat:** 0g	
Protein: 21.3g; **Net Carbs: 18.7g**	
Total Carbs: 23.1g; **Dietary Fiber:** 4.4g; **Sugars:** 5.3g	
Cholesterol: 48mg; **Sodium:** 401mg; **Potassium:** 636mg;	
Vitamin A: 14%; **Vitamin C:** 76%; **Calcium:** 13%; **Iron:** 12%.	

Ingredients:

- ½ large fennel bulb, cored and thinly sliced
- ½ large onion, sliced
- 2 tablespoons olive oil
- 2 trout fillets
- ¼ cup breadcrumbs
- 6 ounces cherry tomatoes, halved
- ¼ cup sliced black olives
- 1 lemon, thinly sliced

Directions:

1. Preheat the oven to 400 degrees F. Line a baking sheet with aluminum foil and grease it with olive oil.
2. Spread the sliced fennel bulb and onion in a layer on the prepared sheet and bake for 10 minutes.
3. Remove from the oven and top the fennel with the fish fillets. Sprinkle with breadcrumbs and top with halved cherry tomatoes, olives and lemon slices.
4. Bake in the oven for another 5 minutes, then broil for another 3 to 5 minutes.

Pasta

Pasta with Artichokes, Olives, and Tomatoes

Prep Time: 15 minutes; **Cook Time:** 10 minutes	
Serving Size: 185g; **Serves:** 4; **Calories:** 465	
Total Fat: 11.3g **Saturated Fat:** 2.3g; **Trans Fat:** 0g	
Protein: 14.8g; **Net Carbs:** 65.1g	
Total Carbs: 69.9g; **Dietary Fiber:** 4.8g; **Sugars:** 3.5g	
Cholesterol: 4mg; **Sodium:** 213mg; **Potassium:** 363mg;	
Vitamin A: 1%; **Vitamin C:** 6%; **Calcium:** 11%; **Iron:** 18%.	

Ingredients:
- 12 ounces whole-wheat spaghetti, dry
- 2 tablespoons olive oil
- ½ medium onion, thinly sliced
- 2 garlic cloves, thinly sliced
- ½ cup dry white wine
- 1 can artichoke hearts, drained, rinsed and quartered lengthwise
- 1/3 cup pitted black olives, quartered
- 1 cup cherry tomatoes, halved
- ¼ cup grated Parmesan cheese

Directions:
1. Cook the spaghetti until al dente. Drain and keep 1 cup of pasta water. Return the cooked spaghetti to the pot.
2. In the meantime, heat 1 tablespoon of olive oil over medium-high, toss in the onion and garlic and cook for 3 to 4 minutes, stirring occasionally. Pour in the wine and cook for another 2 minutes, until the wine evaporates.
3. Stir in the halved artichokes and cook for another 2 to 3 minutes. Toss in the olives and half of the tomatoes. Cook for another 1 or 2 minutes.
4. Stir in the spaghetti, the remaining half of the tomatoes, olive oil and Parmesan cheese.
5. Serve immediately.

Pasta Salad with Feta and Parmesan

Prep Time: 30 minutes; **Cook Time:** 15 minutes
Serving Size: 233g; **Serves:** 6; **Calories:** 431
Total Fat: 13.8g **Saturated Fat:** 4.3g; **Trans Fat:** 0g
Protein: 20.1g; **Net Carbs:** 49.7g
Total Carbs: 60.1g; **Dietary Fiber:** 10.4g; **Sugars:** 2.7g
Cholesterol: 20mg; **Sodium:** 993mg; **Potassium:** 11mg;
Vitamin A: 8%; **Vitamin C:** 4%; **Calcium:** 23%; **Iron:** 23%.

Ingredients:
- [ ] 1 pound tricolor pasta
- [ ] ¼ cup balsamic vinegar
- [ ] 2 teaspoons Dijon mustard
- [ ] 1/2 teaspoon salt
- [ ] 2 tablespoons olive oil
- [ ] 1/3 cup diced sun dried tomatoes
- [ ] 1 (14.5 ounce) can artichoke hearts, drained and diced
- [ ] ¼ cup fresh basil
- [ ] ¼ cup diced red onion
- [ ] ¾ cup black olives, sliced
- [ ] 4 ounces feta cheese, crumbled
- [ ] ½ cup freshly grated Parmesan cheese

Directions:

1. Whisk the balsamic vinegar, mustard and salt in a small bowl. Slowly whisk in the olive oil to make a dressing. Set aside.
2. Prepare the pasta according to directions on the package, rain and transfer to a large bowl. While it is still warm, pour some dressing over it and toss, so it doesn't stick together. Let it cool at room temperature, tossing occasionally.
3. When cool, stir in the sun dried tomatoes, diced artichokes, basil, onion and olives.
4. Pour in the vinaigrette and toss until all the ingredients are evenly coated.
5. Finish off by adding the feta and Parmesan cheese.

Pasta with Zucchini

Prep Time: 10 minutes; **Cook Time:** 15 minutes
Serving Size: 225g; **Serves:** 4; **Calories:** 492
Total Fat: 9.8g **Saturated Fat:** 2g; **Trans Fat:** 0g
Protein: 17.2g; **Net Carbs:** 81.1g
Total Carbs: 86.8g; **Dietary Fiber:** 5g; **Sugars:** 4.3g
Cholesterol: 3mg; **Sodium:** 91mg; **Potassium:** 260mg;
Vitamin A: 4%; **Vitamin C:** 28%; **Calcium:** 9%; **Iron:** 28%.

Ingredients:

- 1 pound rigatoni or any other short pasta, dry
- 2 tablespoons olive oil
- 2 zucchini, chopped
- 1 tablespoon chopped sun dried tomatoes
- 1 tablespoon black olives
- 1 tablespoon capers
- 3 tablespoons Parmesan cheese, freshly grated

Directions:

1. Cook the pasta according to package instructions.
2. In the meantime, heat the oil in a skillet and cook the sliced zucchini until lightly golden.
3. Drain the pasta and keep ½ cup of water it was cooked in.
4. Add pasta, sun dried tomatoes, olives, capers and parmesan cheese to the skillet and gently stir. Add some of the reserved water to loosen the pasta
5. Before serving, sprinkle with some more Parmesan cheese.

Pasta with Eggplant and Pine Kernels

Prep Time: 10 minutes; **Cook Time:** 30 minutes

Serving Size: 380g; **Serves:** 4; **Calories:** 491

Total Fat: 20.7g **Saturated Fat:** 2.4g; **Trans Fat:** 0g

Protein: 12.7g; **Net Carbs:** 57g

Total Carbs: 69.5g; **Dietary Fiber:** 12.5g; **Sugars:** 11.1g

Cholesterol: 0mg; **Sodium:** 7mg; **Potassium:** 698mg;

Vitamin A: 8%; **Vitamin C:** 17%; **Calcium:** 4%; **Iron:** 19%.

Ingredients:

- 10 ounces pasta, dry
- 2 large eggplants
- 4 tablespoons olive oil
- 1 ounce fresh basil leaves
- juice of ½ lemon
- 4 tablespoons pine kernels

Directions:

1. Cut both eggplants in half horizontally, make shallow cuts in a crisscross fashion and brush generously with oil.
2. Grill it for about 20 minutes, until the eggplant becomes soft inside. Scrape the flesh out into a large bowl, pour in 4 tablespoons of olive oil and beat until a smooth sauce forms.
3. Chop up the basil and mix it in, along with lemon juice.
4. Cook the pasta according to package instructions. In the meantime, toast the pine kernels in a non-stick pan.
5. Drain the pasta and serve it with the eggplant sauce, topped with the pine kernels.

Spaghetti with Chorizo

Prep Time: 20 minutes; **Cook Time:** 20 minutes	
Serving Size: 178g; **Serves:** 2; **Calories:** 565	
Total Fat: 22.5g **Saturated Fat:** 5.3g; **Trans Fat:** 0g	
Protein: 21.3g; **Net Carbs:** 67.4g	
Total Carbs: 71.5g; **Dietary Fiber:** 4.1g; **Sugars:** 6.3g	
Cholesterol: 25mg; **Sodium:** 546mg; **Potassium:** 529mg;	
Vitamin A: 10%; **Vitamin C:** 13%; **Calcium:** 3%; **Iron:** 23%.	

Ingredients:
- 6 ounces spaghetti, dry
- 1 tablespoon olive oil
- 1 clove garlic, slivered
- 2 ounces chorizo, cut into strips
- ¼ cups sundried tomato paste
- ¼ cups pitted black olives, chopped
- salt and pepper, to taste

Directions:
1. Cook the spaghetti according to the instructions on the package.
2. Heat the olive oil in a skillet and toss in the slivered garlic and chorizo. Cook for about 1 minute. Mix in the sundried tomato paste and chopped black olives. Cook for another minute.
1. Drain the spaghetti and add them to the sauce. Season with salt and pepper to taste.

Chicken with Penne Pasta

Prep Time: 10 minutes; **Cook Time:** 30 minutes

Serving Size: 208g; **Serves:** 6; **Calories:** 315

Total Fat: 10.1g **Saturated Fat:** 2.9g; **Trans Fat:** 0g

Protein: 26.3g; **Net Carbs:** 25.6g

Total Carbs: 29.8g; **Dietary Fiber:** 4.2g; **Sugars:** 3.6g

Cholesterol: 53mg; **Sodium:** 390mg; **Potassium:** 8mg;

Vitamin A: 7%; **Vitamin C:** 9%; **Calcium:** 6%; **Iron:** 14%.

Ingredients:
- 1 pound boneless, skinless chicken breast, cubed
- 4 garlic cloves, minced
- 1 tablespoon olive oil
- 2 (14.5-ounce) cans diced tomatoes, undrained
- ½ cup black olives, chopped
- 1 teaspoon dried basil
- 1 teaspoon dried oregano
- salt and pepper, to taste
- ⅔ cup crumbled feta cheese
- 8 ounces penne pasta, dry

Directions:
1. Cook the pasta according to the instructions on the package.
2. In the meantime, heat in olive oil in a skillet. Todd in the minced garlic and chicken and cook for about 8 minutes. Transfer the chicken to a separate plate and add the canned tomatoes, chopped olives, basil, oregano, salt and pepper to the same skillet. Let it simmer for 8 to 10 minutes on low heat. Stir frequently.
3. When the sauce thickens, put the chicken back in and stir well. Sprinkle with feta cheese, cover with a lid and let it sit for about 5 minutes.
4. Serve fresh over the pasta.

Greek Vegetarian Pasta

Prep Time: 15 minutes; **Cook Time:** 15 minutes	
Serving Size: 249g; **Serves**: 4; **Calories:** 558	
Total Fat: 17.4g **Saturated Fat**: 3.2g; **Trans Fat**: 0g	
Protein: 17.1g; **Net Carbs:** 82.3g	
Total Carbs: 87.7g; **Dietary Fiber:** 5.4g; **Sugars:** 3.9g	
Cholesterol: 10mg; **Sodium:** 358mg; **Potassium:** 205mg;	
Vitamin A: 2%; **Vitamin C**: 26%; **Calcium**: 3%; **Iron**: 33%.	

Ingredients:
- 2-3 tomatoes, chopped
- ½ cup black olives, chopped
- ½ cup crumbled feta cheese
- 2 tablespoons chopped parsley
- ¼ teaspoon salt
- ¼ teaspoon black pepper
- 1 pound penne pasta, dry
- 3 tablespoons olive oil
- 1 clove garlic, minced

Directions:

1. Combine the chopped tomatoes, olives, feta cheese, parsley, salt and pepper in a large bowl. Set aside.
2. Cook the pasta according to the instructions on the package and drain it.
3. Use the same pot to heat the olive oil. Add the minced garlic and let it cook for about 2 minutes. Toss the pasta back in the pot and coat with the olive oil sauce.
4. Add the pasta in the same bowl with the chopped vegetables and stir well.

Baked Pasta with Shrimp

Prep Time: 15 minutes; **Cook Time:** 20 minutes	
Serving Size: 247g; **Serves:** 4; **Calories:** 411	
Total Fat: 12.7g **Saturated Fat:** 3.8g; **Trans Fat:** 0g	
Protein: 35.3g; **Net Carbs:** 35.3g	
Total Carbs: 38g; **Dietary Fiber:** 2.7g; **Sugars:** 2.5g	
Cholesterol: 229mg; **Sodium:** 895mg; **Potassium:** 383mg;	
Vitamin A: 51%; **Vitamin C:** 90%; **Calcium:** 17%; **Iron:** 37%.	

Ingredients:
- 2 ½ cups farfalle pasta, dry
- 1 pound uncooked medium shrimp, peeled, deveined, tail shells removed
- 4 ounces crumbled feta cheese
- 3 cups lightly packed fresh spinach, chopped
- 1 medium red bell pepper, chopped
- ½ teaspoon salt
- 2 tablespoons olive oil

Directions:
1. Heat the oven to 350 degrees F. Grease a large glass baking dish with olive or vegetable oil.
2. Cook the pasta according to the instructions on the package. Then, 2 minutes before done, add in the shrimp and cook until they turn pink and the pasta is tender. Drain and return to the same pot.
3. Stir the crumbled feta cheese, spinach, bell pepper and salt into the pasta. Pour everything into the prepared baking dish and bake for 10 to 15 minutes.
4. Before serving, sprinkle with 1 tablespoon of olive oil and toss well.

Oven Baked Pasta

Prep Time: 15 minutes; **Cook Time:** 15 minutes
Serving Size: 230g; **Serves:** 4; **Calories:** 196
Total Fat: 7.8g **Saturated Fat:** 2.4g; **Trans Fat:** 0g
Protein: 8g; **Net Carbs:** 20.7g
Total Carbs: 24.8g; **Dietary Fiber:** 4.1g; **Sugars:** 2.9g
Cholesterol: 11mg; **Sodium:** 189mg; **Potassium:** 389mg;
Vitamin A: 2%; **Vitamin C:** 33%; **Calcium:** 11%; **Iron:** 18%.

Ingredients:
- 1 cup cooked pasta
- 3 tomatoes, chopped
- 2 onions, finely sliced
- 3 cloves garlic, slivered
- 1 tablespoon olive oil
- ½ cup cooked or canned chickpeas
- salt and pepper, to taste
- ½ cup shredded mozzarella cheese

Directions:
1. Preheat the oven to 450 degrees F.
2. In a baking dish, layer the slivered garlic, sliced onions and chopped tomatoes. Drizzle with olive oil and bake in oven for about 10 minutes
3. In a separate bowl, stir together the cooked pasta, chickpeas and roasted vegetables. Season with salt and pepper.
4. Cover with mozzarella cheese and bake for another 10 minutes, until the cheese turns golden brown.

Side Dishes

Baked Risotto with Chorizo Sausage

Prep Time: 15 minutes; **Cook Time:** 30 minutes	
Serving Size: 572g; **Serves:** 4; **Calories:** 470	
Total Fat: 10g **Saturated Fat:** 2.9g; **Trans Fat:** 0g	
Protein: 18.6g; **Net Carbs:** 75g	
Total Carbs: 78.4g; **Dietary Fiber:** 3.4g; **Sugars:** 4.4g	
Cholesterol: 31mg; **Sodium:** 1736mg; **Potassium:** 165mg;	
Vitamin A: 11%; **Vitamin C:** 61%; **Calcium:** 16%; **Iron:** 12%.	

Ingredients:
- 1/2 tablespoon olive oil
- 1 leek, finely chopped
- 1 chorizo sausage, finely sliced
- 2 garlic cloves, minced
- 1 teaspoon dried oregano
- 2 cups long grained rice, uncooked
- 6 cups chicken broth
- 8 sun dried tomatoes, finely sliced
- 1/4 cup sliced black olives
- 1 small bunch fresh broccoli, stalks removed
- 1/2 cup finely grated Parmesan cheese

Directions:
1. Heat your oven to 350 degrees F.
2. Heat the olive oil in a cast iron pan on the stovetop, add the chopped leek and chorizo and cook for 2 to 3 minutes.
3. Add in the minced garlic, oregano, rice and 5 ½ cups of the chicken broth. Stir well.
4. Transfer the pan from the stove to the oven and cook for about 20 minutes.
5. Remove from the oven and add the remaining ½ cup of the broth. Then add in the dried tomatoes, olives, broccoli and Parmesan cheese.
6. Return to the oven and bake for 5 to 8 minutes more, until all the liquid evaporates.
7. Before serving, let it sit for about 5 minutes.

Vegetarian Mushroom Risotto

Prep Time: 15 minutes; **Cook Time:** 45 minutes	
Serving Size: 450g; **Serves:** 4; **Calories:** 306	
Total Fat: 10.2g **Saturated Fat:** 2.7g; **Trans Fat:** 0g	
Protein: 8.7g; **Net Carbs:** 44g	
Total Carbs: 44.7g; **Dietary Fiber:** 0.7g; **Sugars:** 2.7g	
Cholesterol: 7mg; **Sodium:** 757mg; **Potassium:** 10mg;	
Vitamin A: 6%; **Vitamin C:** 2%; **Calcium:** 14%; **Iron:** 3%.	

Ingredients:
- 2 tablespoons olive oil
- 1/2 cup minced shallots
- 1 8-ounce package of cremini mushrooms, sliced
- ¼ teaspoon salt
- 1 cup dry Arborio rice
- 1/3 cup dry white wine
- 5 cups vegetable broth
- ½ cup grated Parmesan cheese
- 1/4 cup minced fresh basil

Directions:
1. Preheat the oven to 350 degrees F.
2. Warm 1 tablespoon of olive oil in a Dutch oven. Then add the shallots, cook for about a minute and add the mushrooms. Cook for about 6 to 8 minutes on medium heat.
3. Pour in the rice and stir well. Add the wine and cook until all the liquids have evaporated.
4. Pour in the broth and stir. Cover and place the dish into the oven. Bake for about 45 minutes.
5. When done, remove from the oven, add the other tablespoon of olive oil and grated Parmesan. Stir well.
6. Stir in the fresh basil and serve immediately.

Vegetable Chili

Prep Time: 10 minutes; **Cook Time:** 30 minutes	
Serving Size: 472g; **Serves:** 6; **Calories:** 206	
Total Fat: 7.5g **Saturated Fat:** 1.1g; **Trans Fat:** 0g	
Protein: 8.3g; **Net Carbs:** 19.1g	
Total Carbs: 29.4g; **Dietary Fiber:** 10.3g; **Sugars:** 11.5g	
Cholesterol: 0mg; **Sodium:** 226mg; **Potassium:** 974mg;	
Vitamin A: 71%; **Vitamin C:** 248%; **Calcium:** 8%; **Iron:** 21%.	

Ingredients:
- 3 tablespoons olive oil
- 2 red onions, diced
- 3 medium peppers, diced
- 2 zucchini, diced
- 1 large eggplant, diced
- 2 (14-ounce) cans cherry tomatoes, with juice
- 1 (14-ounce) can kidney beans, drained
- 9 ounces baby spinach

Directions:
1. Toss the olive oil, diced red onions, peppers, zucchinis and eggplant in a large skillet, cover with a lid and cook for about 10 minutes.
2. Pour in the cherry tomatoes and beans and let it simmer for another 15 minutes.
3. Finally, remove from heat and stir in the spinach.

Eggplant and Rice

Prep Time: 10 minutes; **Cook Time:** 42 minutes	
Serving Size: 245g; **Serves:** 6; **Calories:** 143	
Total Fat: 9g **Saturated Fat:** 1g; **Trans Fat:** 0g	
Protein: 3g; **Net Carbs:** 11g	
Total Carbs: 15g; **Dietary Fiber:** 4g; **Sugars:** 4g	
Cholesterol: 0mg; **Sodium:** 175mg; **Potassium:** 290mg;	
Vitamin A: 0%; **Vitamin C**: 11%; **Calcium**: 1%; **Iron**: 13%.	

Ingredients:

- 1 medium eggplant
- ¼ cup olive oil
- 1 large onion, finely chopped
- 1 medium tomato, chopped
- 4-6 garlic cloves, minced
- freshly ground black pepper (to taste)
- 1 teaspoon dried oregano
- 2 teaspoons salt
- 1 bay leaf
- 1 cup long grain rice
- 2 cups chicken or vegetable stock

Directions:

1. Preheat the oven to 400 degrees F.
2. Chop the eggplant into 1 inch pieces.
3. Heat the olive oil in a skillet over medium heat, add the chopped eggplant and stir well.
4. Add the salt and continue to sauté, so the eggplant softens. Then add the onion, garlic and tomato and cook for another minute or so.
5. Season with salt, pepper and oregano.
6. Finish off by adding the rice and bay leaf, then pour in the chicken or vegetable stock.
7. Place the whole thing in the oven and bake for 30 minutes.
8. Remove from the oven and let it cool slightly before serving.

Zucchini Noodles

Prep Time: 10 minutes; **Cook Time:** 10 minutes	
Serving Size: 613g; **Serves:** 2; **Calories:** 253	
Total Fat: 16.1g **Saturated Fat:** 4.7g; **Trans Fat:** 0g	
Protein: 11.4g; **Net Carbs:** 15.5g	
Total Carbs: 22.6g; **Dietary Fiber:** 6.9g; **Sugars:** 7g	
Cholesterol: 20mg; **Sodium:** 670mg; **Potassium:** 1389mg;	
Vitamin A: 42%; **Vitamin C:** 181%; **Calcium:** 14%; **Iron:** 12%.	

Ingredients:
- [ ] 4 zucchini, spiralized
- [ ] 1 tablespoon olive oil
- [ ] 2 garlic cloves, minced
- [ ] 2 cups chopped tomatoes
- [ ] 2 tablespoon capers
- [ ] ¼ cup green olives, halved
- [ ] 1 teaspoon dried oregano
- [ ] 1 tablespoon fresh lemon juice
- [ ] salt and pepper, to taste
- [ ] ⅓ cup thinly sliced fresh basil leaves
- [ ] ½ cup crumbled feta cheese

Directions:
2. Spiralize the zucchini and toss the zucchini noodles in a large bowl.
3. Heat the olive oil in a skillet, add the chopped tomatoes and minced garlic and sauté for about 5 minutes.
4. Mix in the capers, olives, oregano, lemon juice and season with salt and pepper. Let it cook for an additional 5 minutes.
5. Pour the sauce over the zucchini noodles and sprinkle with basil leaves and crumbled feta cheese.
6. Serve right away.

Quick Chickpea Stew

Prep Time: 10 minutes; **Cook Time:** 10 minutes
Serving Size: 652g; **Serves:** 2; **Calories:** 390
Total Fat: 14.1g **Saturated Fat:** 1.3g; **Trans Fat:** 0g
Protein: 15.5g; **Net Carbs:** 39.2g
Total Carbs: 54.4g; **Dietary Fiber:** 15.2g; **Sugars:** 5g
Cholesterol: 0mg; **Sodium:** 749mg; **Potassium:** 1477mg;
Vitamin A: 3%; **Vitamin C:** 241%; **Calcium:** 18%; **Iron:** 62%.

Ingredients:

- 2 cups chickpeas, drained and rinsed
- 4 medium tomatoes, chopped
- 1 small zucchini, chopped
- 1 small onion, chopped
- 1 bell pepper, striped
- 2 garlic cloves, minced
- 1 tablespoon olive oil
- 1 teaspoon sesame seeds
- 10 fresh basil leaves, chopped

Directions:

1. Mix the tomatoes and onion in a large pan, cover with a lid and let it simmer for about 3 to 4 minutes.
2. Add the chickpeas, stir, cover with a lid and let it simmer for another 5 minutes.
3. Add the minced garlic, chopped zucchini and bell pepper. Stir well and cook for 2 more minutes.
4. Remove from heat, add fresh basil leaves and olive oil. Sprinkle with sesame seeds.

Simple Oven Baked Vegetables

Prep Time: 5 minutes; **Cook Time:** 35 minutes	
Serving Size: 465g; **Serves:** 2; **Calories:** 113	
Total Fat: 3g **Saturated Fat:** 0.5g; **Trans Fat:** 0g	
Protein: 5.2g; **Net Carbs:** 14.3g	
Total Carbs: 19.6g; **Dietary Fiber:** 5.3g; **Sugars:** 13.2g	
Cholesterol: 0mg; **Sodium:** 23mg; **Potassium:** 1112mg;	
Vitamin A: 16%; **Vitamin C:** 125%; **Calcium:** 6%; **Iron:** 9%.	

Ingredients:
- olive oil, for greasing
- 1 large red onion, cut into 1/4-inch wedges
- 2 medium zucchini, sliced diagonally
- 2 yellow crookneck squash, sliced diagonally
- salt and pepper, to taste
- 2 tablespoons balsamic vinegar
- 1 teaspoon olive oil

Directions:
1. Preheat the oven to 400 degrees F. Grease a baking sheet with olive oil and spread all the prepared vegetables on it.
2. Season with salt and pepper and drizzle over the balsamic vinegar and olive oil.
3. Bake for 35 minutes, stirring occasionally.

Baked Vegetables with Feta Cheese

Prep Time: 5 minutes; **Cook Time:** 25 minutes
Serving Size: 146g; **Serves:** 4; **Calories:** 174
Total Fat: 14g **Saturated Fat:** 3.8g; **Trans Fat:** 0g
Protein: 4.3g; **Net Carbs:** 8.1g
Total Carbs: 10.3g; **Dietary Fiber:** 2.2g; **Sugars:** 4.3g
Cholesterol: 15mg; **Sodium:** 152mg; **Potassium:** 213mg;
Vitamin A: 4%; **Vitamin C:** 230%; **Calcium:** 9%; **Iron:** 17%.

Ingredients:

- 1 medium onion, roughly chopped
- 3 small bell peppers, roughly chopped
- 2 small zucchini, roughly chopped
- 5 garlic cloves, slivered
- ½ tsp dried oregano
- salt and pepper, to taste
- 3 tablespoons olive oil
- lemon juice, to taste
- 4 tablespoons crumbled feta cheese

Directions:

1. Preheat the oven to 450 degrees F.
2. Toss the onion, peppers, zucchini and garlic into a baking dish. Season with salt and pepper to taste. Drizzle with olive oil and stir.
3. Bake in the oven for 25 minutes, stirring once.
4. Before serving, sprinkle with lemon juice and crumbled feta cheese.

Roasted Asparagus

Prep Time: 5 minutes; **Cook Time:** 15 minutes

Serving Size: 248g; **Serves:** 4; **Calories:** 118

Total Fat: 7.5g **Saturated Fat:** 1.8g; **Trans Fat:** 0g

Protein: 5.7g; **Net Carbs:** 6g

Total Carbs: 9.3g; **Dietary Fiber:** 3.3g; **Sugars:** 4.7g

Cholesterol: 5mg; **Sodium:** 432mg; **Potassium:** 514mg;

Vitamin A: 42%; **Vitamin C:** 42%; **Calcium:** 8%; **Iron:** 6%.

Ingredients:
- 12 ounces asparagus (trimmed)
- 1 tablespoon olive oil
- 6 cherry tomatoes, halved
- 2 ounces crumbled feta cheese
- 12 green olives

Directions:
1. Preheat the oven to 400 degrees F.
2. Pour 1 tablespoon of olive oil on a baking sheet.
3. Roll the asparagus in the oil and bake in the oven for 12 minutes.
4. Remove from the oven, add the cherry tomatoes and bake for another 3 minutes.
5. Before serving, sprinkle with crumbled feta cheese and olives.

Salads

Grilled Chicken Salad

Prep Time: 20 minutes; Cook Time: 10 minutes	
Serving Size: 324g; Serves: 4; Calories: 495	
Total Fat: 27.3g Saturated Fat: 6.4g; Trans Fat: 0g	
Protein: 25.8g; Net Carbs: 16.1g	
Total Carbs: 22.6g; Dietary Fiber: 6.5g; Sugars: 2.2g	
Cholesterol: 47mg; Sodium: 1387mg; Potassium: 639mg;	
Vitamin A: 7%; Vitamin C: 67%; Calcium: 22%; Iron: 21%.	

Ingredients:
- 3 tablespoons lemon juice, divided
- 3 tablespoons olive oil, divided
- 1 tablespoon minced garlic, divided
- 1 teaspoon salt, divided
- 2 boned, skinned chicken breast halves
- 2 tablespoons tahini
- 2 (15-ounce) cans chickpeas, drained and rinsed
- 2 tomatoes, chopped
- ½ red onion, thinly sliced
- ½ red bell pepper, sliced
- 6 ounces feta cheese, crumbled

Directions:

1. Heat the grill to high and mix 1 tablespoon of lemon juice and olive oil, 1 teaspoon of garlic, and 1/2 teaspoon of salt. Coat the chicken in the mixture.
2. Grill the chicken for about 10 minutes, turning once. Remove from the grill, cover and let it rest for about 5 minutes.
3. Mix together the remaining lemon juice, olive oil, minced garlic, salt and tahini. Toss in the chickpeas, chopped tomatoes, sliced onion and bell pepper.
4. Divide the salad among 4 plates and serve with sliced chicken breasts and crumbled feta cheese on top.

Orzo Salad

Prep Time: 40 minutes; Cook Time: 10 minutes
Serving Size: 303g; Serves: 4; Calories: 329
Total Fat: 15.9g Saturated Fat: 3.3g; Trans Fat: 0g
Protein: 9.8g; Net Carbs: 35.2g
Total Carbs: 39.5g; Dietary Fiber: 4.3g; Sugars: 6.1g
Cholesterol: 10mg; Sodium: 257mg; Potassium: 325mg;
Vitamin A: 13%; Vitamin C: 76%; Calcium: 7%; Iron: 12%.

Ingredients:
- 6 ounces orzo pasta
- 3 tablespoons olive oil
- red wine vinegar, to taste
- 2 whole cucumbers, sliced
- ½ cup black olives, halved
- ½ cup cherry tomatoes, halved
- 2 small green peppers, diced
- ½ cup crumbled feta cheese

Directions:
1. Cook the pasta according to package instructions. Meanwhile, chop up the vegetables.
2. Drain the pasta and toss it in a large bowl. Stir in the vegetables, olive oil and a few splashes of red wine vinegar.
3. Cover with tin foil and let it cool in the fridge for about 30 minutes.
4. Before serving, slowly fold in the crumbled feta cheese as well.

Rice Salad with Feta Cheese

Prep Time: 10 minutes; **Cook Time:** 20 minutes
Serving Size: 295g; **Serves:** 4; **Calories:** 437
Total Fat: 23.6g **Saturated Fat:** 6.7g; **Trans Fat:** 0g
Protein: 11.8g; **Net Carbs:** 46.5g
Total Carbs: 49.8g; **Dietary Fiber:** 3.3g; **Sugars:** 5.3g
Cholesterol: 27mg; **Sodium:** 504mg; **Potassium:** 167mg;
Vitamin A: 17%; **Vitamin C:** 46%; **Calcium:** 11%; **Iron:** 6%.

Ingredients:
- 1 ⅛ cups rice
- 1 ⅓ cups cherry tomatoes, halved
- ⅓ cup black olives, roughly chopped
- 2 scallions, cut into rings
- 1 cucumber, peeled and diced
- 1 ⅓ cups crumbled feta cheese
- 4 tablespoons lemon juice
- 1 teaspoon honey
- 4 tablespoons olive oil
- salt and pepper, to taste

Directions:
1. Cook the rice according to the instructions on the package and let in cool completely.
2. In a large serving bowl, mix all the prepared vegetables and crumbled feta cheese. Toss in the prepared rice as well.
3. Add the lemon juice, honey and oil in the same bowl and gently stir. Season with salt and pepper to taste.

Classic Mediterranean Potato Salad

Prep Time: 25 minutes; **Cook Time:** 25 minutes
Serving Size: 215g; **Serves:** 6; **Calories:** 270
Total Fat: 14.4g **Saturated Fat:** 1.6g; **Trans Fat:** 0g
Protein: 3.5g; **Net Carbs:** 27.5g
Total Carbs: 30.3g; **Dietary Fiber:** 2.8g; **Sugars:** 2.5g
Cholesterol: 0mg; **Sodium:** 196mg; **Potassium:** 818mg;
Vitamin A: 0%; **Vitamin C:** 32%; **Calcium:** 2%; **Iron:** 6%.

Ingredients:

- 2 pounds round red potatoes
- salt, to taste
- 1/3 cup olive oil
- 3 tablespoons white wine vinegar
- 1 ½ cups black olives, roughly chopped
- 1/3 cup chopped red onion
- black pepper, to taste

Directions:

1. Place the the potatoes in a large pan, cover with 1 inch of water, season with salt, cover with a lid and bring to a boil. Then, uncover, reduce the heat and let it simmer for about 15 minutes, until the potatoes are perfectly tender.
2. Once they are slightly chilled, cut them into small chunks, remove the skin and transfer them to a large serving bowl.
3. In a separate, smaller bowl, mix together the oil, white wine vinegar, black olives and onion. Season with black pepper to taste.
4. Pour the dressing over the potatoes and toss well.
5. Serve at room temperature.

Couscous Salad with Feta Cheese

Prep Time: 15 minutes; **Cook Time:** 5 minutes
Serving Size: 253g; **Serves:** 4; **Calories:** 255
Total Fat: 5.5g **Saturated Fat:** 2.6g; **Trans Fat:** 0g
Protein: 11.2g; **Net Carbs:** 39.6g
Total Carbs: 43.5g; **Dietary Fiber:** 3.9g; **Sugars:** 4g
Cholesterol: 15mg; **Sodium:** 265mg; **Potassium:** 294mg;
Vitamin A: 7%; **Vitamin C:** 30%; **Calcium:** 6%; **Iron:** 16%.

Ingredients:
- ¼ cup white wine vinegar
- 4 teaspoons fresh lemon juice
- 1 cup whole wheat couscous, dry
- ½ red onion, diced
- 1 medium cucumber, peeled and chopped
- 2 large tomatoes, chopped
- ¾ cup crumbled feta cheese
- 1 teaspoon garlic powder
- salt and pepper, to taste
- 2 tablespoons balsamic vinegar

Directions:
1. Boil 1 ¼ cups of water in a medium pot. Add the couscous, cover with a lid and remove from the heat. Let it sit.
2. In the meantime, dice and mix together the onion, cucumbers and tomatoes.
3. In a separate bowl, mix the white wine vinegar and lemon juice and heat it slightly in the microwave.
4. Stir the couscous with a fork and transfer it into a serving bowl.
5. Toss in the vegetables, feta cheese and garlic powder. Pour in the white wine dressing and stir well. Season with salt and pepper to taste.
6. Before serving, drizzle with balsamic vinegar.

Crunchy Broccoli Salad

Prep Time: 70 minutes; **Cook Time:** 0 minutes

Serving Size: 594g; **Serves:** 2; **Calories:** 293

Total Fat: 5g **Saturated Fat:** 4g; **Trans Fat:** 0.1g

Protein: 15.1g; **Net Carbs:** 35.5g

Total Carbs: 48.5g; **Dietary Fiber:** 13g; **Sugars:** 7.7g

Cholesterol: 0mg; **Sodium:** 739mg; **Potassium:** 1307mg;

Vitamin A: 122%; **Vitamin C:** 171%; **Calcium:** 25%; **Iron:** 24%.

Ingredients:
- 1 (15-ounce) can chickpeas, drained
- 1 cucumber, chopped
- 1 cup small broccoli florets
- 1 cup grape tomatoes, halved
- 1 cup finely sliced kale, stems removed
- ½ cup finely chopped red onion
- 2 tablespoons finely chopped black olives
- 3 tablespoons red wine vinegar
- 1 clove garlic, minced

Directions:
1. Toss all the ingredients in a large serving bowl and stir well.
2. Best served nicely chilled for at least 1 hour.

Tuna Salad

Prep Time: 10 minutes; **Cook Time:** 0 minutes	
Serving Size: 358g; **Serves:** 2; **Calories:** 252	
Total Fat: 2.9g **Saturated Fat:** 0.4g; **Trans Fat:** 0g	
Protein: 45.2g; **Net Carbs:** 7.4g	
Total Carbs: 8.9g; **Dietary Fiber:** 1.5g; **Sugars:** 7.1g	
Cholesterol: 51mg; **Sodium:** 654mg; **Potassium:** 658mg;	
Vitamin A: 25%; **Vitamin C:** 85%; **Calcium:** 10%; **Iron:** 19%.	

Ingredients:
- ½ cup tomato-vegetable juice
- 4 tablespoons horseradish mustard
- 2 (6-ounce) cans tuna, packed in water, drained
- 2/3 cup chopped roasted pepper
- 4 tablespoons chopped parsley
- 2 tablespoons chopped black olives

Directions:
1. In a medium bowl, mix together the tomato juice and mustard. Add the tuna, roasted pepper, parsley and olives. Stir well and chill before serving.

Baked Shrimp Salad

Prep Time: 10 minutes; **Cook Time:** 30 minutes

Serving Size: 295g; **Serves:** 4; **Calories:** 287

Total Fat: 17.3g **Saturated Fat:** 2.8g; **Trans Fat:** 0g

Protein: 25.7g; **Net Carbs:** 8.4g

Total Carbs: 9.9g; **Dietary Fiber:** 1.5g; **Sugars:** 0.9g

Cholesterol: 221mg; **Sodium:** 276mg; **Potassium:** 248mg;

Vitamin A: 7%; **Vitamin C:** 28%; **Calcium:** 5%; **Iron:** 31%.

Ingredients:
- ½ cups Italian vinaigrette dressing
- 2 tomatoes, cut into wedges
- 1 cup fennel
- 1 zucchini, chopped
- 2 shallots, sliced
- 1 clove garlic, minced
- 1 pound large shrimp
- 1 tablespoon lemon juice
- 8 cups rocket leaves

Directions:
1. Preheat the oven to 425 degrees F.
2. Toss half of the dressing with the tomato wedges, fennel, chopped zucchini, shallots and garlic in a pan. Roast for about 25 minutes.
3. Stir in the shrimp and lemon juice. Roast for another 5 minutes.
4. In a large bowl, toss the rockets leaves and the other half of the dressing.
5. Serve the shrimp over the salad.

Celery Olive Salad

Prep Time: 70 minutes; **Cook Time:** 0 minutes	
Serving Size: 153g; **Serves:** 6; **Calories:** 211	
Total Fat: 14.1g **Saturated Fat:** 1.6g; **Trans Fat:** 0g	
Protein: 1.5g; **Net Carbs:** 17.7g	
Total Carbs: 21.1g; **Dietary Fiber:** 3.4g; **Sugars:** 16.5g	
Cholesterol: 0mg; **Sodium:** 409mg; **Potassium:** 436mg;	
Vitamin A: 17%; **Vitamin C:** 14%; **Calcium:** 5%; **Iron:** 4%.	

Ingredients:
- 4 cups celery, sliced
- 1 cup green olives, chopped
- 1/3 cup black olives, minced into a fine mixture
- 2 packed cups baby arugula, roughly chopped
- 2 teaspoons Italian seasoning
- ½ cup dried apricots, chopped
- ½ cup dates, chopped
- 1/3 cup olive oil
- juice and zest of 1 lemon

Directions:
1. In a large bowl, toss together the celery, green olives, minced black olives, arugula, Italian seasoning, dried apricots and dates. Stir very well.
2. In a small bowl, stir the olive oil, lemon juice and zest. Drizzle on the salad and toss well.
3. Refrigerate for 1 hour before serving.

Desserts

Grilled Peaches with Yogurt and Honey

Prep Time: 5 minutes; **Cook Time:** 5 minutes
Serving Size: 175g; **Serves:** 4; **Calories:** 134
Total Fat: 0g **Saturated Fat:** 0g; **Trans Fat:** 0g
Protein: 6.6g; **Net Carbs:** 65g
Total Carbs: 30.5g; **Dietary Fiber:** 2g; **Sugars:** 28.5g
Cholesterol: 4mg; **Sodium:** 21mg; **Potassium:** 261mg;
Vitamin A: 2%; **Vitamin C:** 10%; **Calcium:** 6%; **Iron:** 1%.

Ingredients:
- 4 ripe peaches, sliced in half
- 1 cup Greek yogurt
- 4 tablespoons honey
- 1 teaspoon cinnamon

Directions:
1. Place the peaches face down on a grill and grill for 4 to 5 minutes per side.
2. Meanwhile, mix together the yogurt and honey.
3. Remove the peaches from the grill, fill each half with 1 tablespoon of the yogurt mixture and sprinkle with cinnamon.

Fruit Salad

Prep Time: 10 minutes; **Cook Time:** 0 minutes
Serving Size: 331g; **Serves:** 4; **Calories:** 256
Total Fat: 3.8g **Saturated Fat:** 0.3g; **Trans Fat:** 0g
Protein: 8.4g; **Net Carbs:** 49.3g
Total Carbs: 53.3g; **Dietary Fiber:** 4g; **Sugars:** 48.7g
Cholesterol: 4mg; **Sodium:** 36mg; **Potassium:** 312mg;
Vitamin A: 18%; **Vitamin C:** 10%; **Calcium:** 9%; **Iron:** 7%.

Ingredients:
- 4 cups mixed fresh fruit, chopped (grapes, melon, oranges, peaches, berries)
- ¼ cup slivered almonds
- 1 cup plain Greek yogurt
- 3 tablespoons honey
- 1 tablespoon grated lemon rind

Directions:
1. In serving bowl, Stir together the mixed fruits and almonds in a large bowl and set aside.
2. In a smaller bowl, mix the yogurt and honey.
3. In a separate bowl combine yogurt, honey and lemon rind.
4. Serve in four individual serving bowls. First fill them with fruit salad, then spoon over the honey yogurt mixture and sprinkle with some more slivered almonds.

Greek Yogurt with Walnuts

Prep Time: 5 minutes; **Cook Time:** 0 minutes	
Serving Size: 130g; **Serves:** 8; **Calories:** 259	
Total Fat: 15g **Saturated Fat:** 1.5g; **Trans Fat:** 0g	
Protein: 12.1g; **Net Carbs:** 22.3g	
Total Carbs: 23.8g; **Dietary Fiber:** 1.5g; **Sugars:** 21.5g	
Cholesterol: 6mg; **Sodium:** 31mg; **Potassium:** 101mg;	
Vitamin A: 0%; **Vitamin C:** 0%; **Calcium:** 14%; **Iron:** 2%.	

Ingredients:
- ☐ 3 cups plain Greek yogurt
- ☐ ¾ teaspoon vanilla
- ☐ 1 ½ cups toasted walnuts, chopped
- ☐ ½ cup honey

Directions:
1. Mix together the Greek yogurt and vanilla in a large bowl.
2. In 4 individual serving glasses, alternate layers of Greek yogurt, chopped walnuts and honey.

Greek Yogurt with Strawberries

Prep Time: 5 minutes; **Cook Time:** 5 minutes	
Serving Size: 140g; **Serves**: 4; **Calories:** 159	
Total Fat: 4.6g **Saturated Fat**: 0.3g; **Trans Fat**: 0g	
Protein: 7.9g; **Net Carbs:** 22.8g	
Total Carbs: 24.5g; **Dietary Fiber:** 1.7g; **Sugars:** 22.2g	
Cholesterol: 4mg; **Sodium:** 21mg; **Potassium**: 112mg;	
Vitamin A: 0%; **Vitamin C:** 53%; **Calcium:** 8%; **Iron**: 3%.	

Ingredients:
- 8 ounces plain Greek yogurt
- 4 tablespoons honey
- 12 strawberries, roughly chopped
- 4 tablespoons chopped walnuts

Directions:

1. Spoon the yogurt in 4 serving glasses and drizzle each one with 1 tablespoon of honey. Layer chopped strawberries on top of that and sprinkle with walnuts.

Broiled Figs with Greek Yogurt

Prep Time: 5 minutes; **Cook Time:** 5 minutes

Serving Size: 218g; **Serves:** 4; **Calories:** 152

Total Fat: 0g **Saturated Fat:** 0g; **Trans Fat:** 0g

Protein: 11.7g; **Net Carbs:** 23.6g

Total Carbs: 26.3g; **Dietary Fiber:** 2.7g; **Sugars:** 15g

Cholesterol: 8mg; **Sodium:** 40mg; **Potassium:** 120mg;

Vitamin A: 3%; **Vitamin C:** 4%; **Calcium:** 16%; **Iron:** 1%.

Ingredients:
- 8 fresh figs, stemmed and sliced in half
- 1 tablespoon sugar
- 2 cups plain Greek yogurt

Directions:
1. Place the figs in a baking dish cut side up. Sprinkle them with sugar and broil for about 5 minutes.
2. Spoon the yogurt in 4 serving glasses and place the broiled figs on top.
3. Serve right away.

Fruit Salad with Banana Dressing

Prep Time: 15 minutes; **Cook Time:** 0 minutes
Serving Size: 166g; **Serves:** 8; **Calories:** 96
Total Fat: 0.4g **Saturated Fat:** 0g; **Trans Fat:** 0g
Protein: 2.5g; **Net Carbs:** 20g
Total Carbs: 23.1g; **Dietary Fiber:** 3.1g; **Sugars:** 19.1g
Cholesterol: 0mg; **Sodium:** 14mg; **Potassium:** 287mg;
Vitamin A: 17%; **Vitamin C:** 82%; **Calcium:** 3%; **Iron:** 3%.

Ingredients:
- 2 cups pineapple chunks
- 1 cup cantaloupe melon, cubed
- 1 cup honeydew melon, cubed
- 1 cup blackberries
- 1 cup strawberries, sliced
- 1 cup red grapes, seedless
- 1 apple, diced
- 2 bananas, sliced
- ½ cup plain Greek yogurt
- 2 tablespoons honey

Directions:
1. Combine all the fruits, except for bananas, in a large bowl.
2. Place the sliced bananas, yogurt and honey in a food processor and blend until perfectly smooth.
3. Place the fruit salad into 8 individual serving cups and pour the banana dressing over each of them.

Greek Yogurt with Cranberries and Nuts

Prep Time: 5 minutes; **Cook Time:** 5 minutes	
Serving Size: 314g; **Serves**: 2; **Calories:** 311	
Total Fat: 13.3g **Saturated Fat**: 1.3g; **Trans Fat**: 0g	
Protein: 14.7g; **Net Carbs:** 30.6g	
Total Carbs: 36g; **Dietary Fiber:** 5.4g; **Sugars:** 22.8g	
Cholesterol: 8mg; **Sodium**: 41mg; **Potassium:** 244mg;	
Vitamin A: 0%; **Vitamin C**: 106%; **Calcium:** 17%; **Iron:** 6%.	

Ingredients:
- 2 cups fresh cranberries
- ½ cup orange juice
- 4 teaspoons sugar
- 1/3 cup unsalted mixed nuts (cashews, walnuts, hazelnuts, almonds)
- 1 cup plain Greek yogurt

Directions:
1. Toss the cranberries, orange juice and sugar in a saucepan and cook for about 5 minutes, while stirring frequently. The cranberries should pop.
2. In the meantime, heat another pan, toss in the mixed nuts and toast them.
3. Divide the cranberry sauce into two serving cups and pour the Greek yogurt over each of them. Sprinkle with toasted nuts.

7-Day Meal Plan

Day 1: BREAKFAST

Egg Omelet from the Oven

Prep Time: 5 minutes; **Cook Time:** 25 minutes
Serving Size: 248g; **Serves**: 4; **Calories:** 286

LUNCH

Grilled Chicken Salad

Prep Time: 20 minutes; **Cook Time:** 10 minutes
Serving Size: 324g; **Serves**: 4; **Calories:** 495

DINNER

Vegetarian Zucchini Casserole

Prep Time: 20 minutes; **Cook Time:** 40 minutes
Serving Size: 802g; **Serves**: 4; **Calories:** 411

Day 2

BREAKFAST

Spinach Frittata

Prep Time: 10 minutes; **Cook Time:** 7 minutes
Serving Size: 150g; **Serves**: 4; **Calories:** 183

LUNCH

Panera Mediterranean Veggie Sandwich

Prep Time: 15 minutes; **Cook Time:** 0 minutes
Serving Size: 863g; **Serves**: 2; **Calories:** 506

DINNER

Oven Baked Halibut

Prep Time: 10 minutes; **Cook Time:** 20 minutes
Serving Size: 472g; **Serves**: 4; **Calories:** 509

Day 3
BREAKFAST
Peanut Butter Banana Yogurt Bowl

Prep Time: 5 minutes; **Cook Time:** 5 minutes
Serving Size: 308g; **Serves:** 4; **Calories:** 305

LUNCH
Chicken Sandwich

Prep Time: 4 hours; **Cook Time:** 30 minutes
Serving Size: 363g; **Serves:** 4; **Calories:** 504

DINNER
Pappardelle with Red Mullet

Prep Time: 5 minutes; **Cook Time:** 25 minutes
Serving Size: 357g; **Serves:** 5; **Calories:** 503

Day 4
BREAKFAST
Blueberry Quinoa

Prep Time: 5 minutes; **Cook Time:** 5 minutes
Serving Size: 262g; **Serves:** 4; **Calories:** 234

LUNCH
Avocado Tuna Sandwich

Prep Time: 20 minutes; **Cook Time:** 0 minutes
Serving Size: 307g; **Serves:** 4; **Calories:** 430

DINNER

Simple Mediterranean Salmon

Prep Time: 8 minutes; **Cook Time:** 22 minutes
Serving Size: 403g; **Serves:** 4; **Calories:** 448

Day 5
BREAKFAST
Egg Muffins with Vegetables and Parmesan Cheese

Prep Time: 20 minutes; **Cook Time:** 20 minutes
Serving Size: 192g; **Serves:** 2; **Calories:** 218

LUNCH
Rice Salad with Feta Cheese

Prep Time: 10 minutes; **Cook Time:** 20 minutes
Serving Size: 295g; **Serves:** 4; **Calories:** 437

DINNER
Swordfish with Tomatoes

Prep Time: 5 minutes; **Cook Time:** 30 minutes
Serving Size: 368g; **Serves:** 4; **Calories:** 408

Day 6
BREAKFAST
Baked Eggs from Tuscany

Prep Time: 5 minutes; **Cook Time:** 20 minutes
Serving Size: 338g; **Serves:** 2; **Calories:** 277

LUNCH
Orzo Salad

Prep Time: 40 minutes; **Cook Time:** 10 minutes
Serving Size: 303g; **Serves:** 4; **Calories:** 329